Praise for *The Learning I*

An informative and entertaining read, *The Learning Imperative* is a timeless classic that should be on the bookshelf of anyone interested in progressive management. Mark and Andy display a subtleness in their writing with their thoughtful, realistic approach – reminding us all of the importance of learning in any organisation.

Steve Pegram, Chief Operating Officer, Bardel Entertainment

Developing learning organisations is not easy. For this reason, *The Learning Imperative* is an essential read for any leader. The authors' unpacking of how to improve learning and bring about a shared clarity in a team is delivered through insightful and practical strategies, and is complemented by thought-provoking questions to reflect on from beginning to end.

The book also recognises there are many challenges ahead, and that raising performance in any organisation will not happen overnight. But it categorically will not happen if you don't start! Start now, using *The Learning Imperative* as your indispensable guide.

Stuart Allen, Head Teacher, Mile Cross Primary School

I am usually put off business books as they tend to be too academic for my liking; however, I was pleasantly surprised by how enjoyable *The Learning Imperative* is to read and follow. Set out in a logical format, the book is well structured and includes further sources of information at the end of each chapter – thus signposting the reader to delve deeper into the subject if interested.

I recognise many of the identified challenges and barriers that prevent teams and organisations from learning and developing, and these issues are brought to life by the inclusion of relevant examples and case studies from real-life contexts. The case studies are particularly useful as they prompt reflection on how things can be seen and done differently, and they also make the tools and techniques suggested by the authors easier to understand, remember and hence apply.

Practical, well-constructed and full of insightful tips, *The Learning Imperative* is a book that I will continue to refer back to.

Martin Riley, Managing Director, Medway Community Healthcare CIC

The Learning Imperative is practical, easy to read, thought provoking and full of useful anecdotes and examples; it shows that the authors clearly have vast experience in the fields of learning and personal development.

It will help all leaders to get the most out of their teams and, at the same time, make the learning enjoyable and interesting.

Mike McKenna, Solicitor and Partner, Hill Dickinson LLP

The Learning Imperative is a compelling argument for the importance of learning in the workplace and offers a sophisticated yet practical guide to implementing a positive learning culture.

The book has two vital ingredients: plenty of academic substance that is easy to digest, and a writing style that is straightforward and enjoyable to engage with. The real-life examples and case studies are informative and insightful, and promote reflection and understanding. The format of each chapter is excellent too, starting with an outline of the subject under discussion before succinctly delivering the message and wrapping up with action points. The message sticks.

If you are serious about improving performance through learning in the workplace, *The Learning Imperative* delivers key strategies for achieving this in spades.

Luke Fisher, Chief Executive, Steribottle Ltd

As a manager, one is always meant to be looking at new ways to inspire, motivate and lead. What *The Learning Imperative* does in a concise and well-considered way is to make leaders look at their attitude to learning and development and reflect on how they can deliver more effective leadership.

The book clearly describes why learning and development is necessary and sets out how to support the development of future leaders, while also providing very useful step-by-step guidance to assist with implementation. I particularly enjoyed the clear structure of each chapter, with entertaining, relevant anecdotes complemented by illuminating case studies that draw out the key lessons. Each section is followed by prompts for reflection, which serve to question the reader's position on a particular area and to reinforce the points made.

As part of the senior management team of a rapidly growing organisation, I recognise many of the examples given as to how and why learning and development can fail. On this subject Mark and Andy capture, in an entertaining manner, the pitfalls surrounding poorly conceived training – and how learning and development, when properly researched and planned, can be delivered in an effective way. In writing *The Learning Imperative* they have compiled a very informative and practical guide which shows how to implement a successful learning programme that will help to deliver marginal gains.

Mark Nevin, Chief Financial Officer, Portman Travel Group

The Learning Imperative provides a fascinating and wide-ranging summary of both theory and practice in the field of learning and development, offering a compelling narrative on how to improve corporate performance through learning. I've picked up a number of key ideas which I'll take back to the office.

Matt Cuhls, Chief Executive Officer, ReAssure Group

Mark did some consultancy work with our organisation a couple of years ago; the theories and concepts that he discussed were inspirational and changed my approach to learning design forever. Everything he shared then, and more, is included in *The Learning Imperative*.

Containing practical guidance on how to develop performance through effective learning, this book brings the subject to life through case study examples, reflection questions and supporting resources. Furthermore, the strategies shared are straightforward, uncomplicated and easy to implement. You'll wonder how you ever got by without them.

Whether you're a manager, leader, trainer or teacher, *The Learning Imperative* provides plenty of opportunity for self-reflection and growth – see where the journey takes you.

Catherine Blackburn, Learning and Development Lead –
North Region, Next plc

The Learning Imperative is for anyone who wants to motivate their team to grow and perform well. The authors set out very clearly that learning is at the heart of this process – and that if you get the learning right, the rest will follow. But they acknowledge that this is not necessarily an easy (or straightforward) process. Haven't we all asked at one time or another – when things feel tough – whether anyone else is in the same boat as us, or, if we are alone in our struggle, whether everyone else is finding it easy? *The Learning Imperative* helps you tackle such questions head-on. It starts from the premise that members of effective teams must have an 'open-to-learning mindset', and makes you think about how to cultivate and maintain this mindset.

The book will work best if you're willing to reflect and be honest with yourself. Where are you now? What are you trying to achieve? How will you get to where you want to go? Reflection isn't necessarily an easy process, and it sometimes feels a little close to the bone! But the authors guide you through the process via a set of real-life examples, which help you to understand and apply what you learn, and prompt you to think about why and how you do what you do, how you can implement change successfully, and how you can help others learn.

The Learning Imperative is also a caring book. The authors acknowledge that there is life beyond work, and that all leaders, teams and contexts are different. It invites you to think about what you're doing, but doesn't demand that you dedicate every spare moment to it!

It's a practical resource that you can come back to again and again, and use in a range of contexts and in a variety of different ways – I'll be returning to it for a while yet.

Dr Niki Kaiser, Network Research Lead,
Norwich Research School at Notre Dame High School

Raising performance in
organisations by improving learning

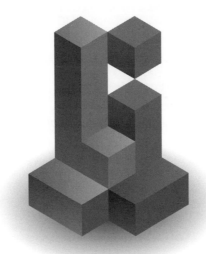

the
learning
imperative

Mark Burns and Andy Griffith

Crown House Publishing Limited
www.crownhouse.co.uk

First published by

Crown House Publishing
Crown Buildings, Bancyfelin, Carmarthen, Wales, SA33 5ND, UK
www.crownhouse.co.uk
and
Crown House Publishing Company LLC
PO Box 2223, Williston, VT 05495, USA
www.crownhousepublishing.com

First published 2018. Reprinted 2019.

British Library Cataloguing-in-Publication Data
A catalogue entry for this book is available
from the British Library.

Print ISBN 978-178583269-7
Mobi ISBN 978-178583375-5
ePub ISBN 978-178583376-2
ePDF ISBN 978-178583377-9

LCCN 2018952790

Edited by Nick Owen

Printed and bound in the UK by
TJ International, Padstow, Cornwall

Foreword

I'm an incorrigible learner; I love the thrill of discovery and the challenge of new disciplines.

My wife despairs of my ever-expanding list of hobbies – running, cycling, mountain biking, sailing, photography, kayaking (and the rest) – and the growing pile of kit in the garage that inevitably accompanies these endeavours.

My career has followed a similar pattern. Having led a couple of geography departments through successful Ofsted inspections, I qualified as an accountant with KPMG and worked in the dark arts of corporate recovery. I then moved on to work for a FTSE 100 software business in a variety of roles, including international posts in which quickly learning your brief was critical to effective engagement with local teams. Right now I'm working on the executive team of a leading housing association intent on tackling the housing crisis head-on.

Incredible then for a learner like me that it took reading Mark and Andy's book for it to really hit home how critical learning is for an organisation's success. The headlines concerning *The Learning Imperative* are, of course, all about learning, but don't let them fool you: this book is not only about learning but also about how to make teams work, how to lead and how to create cultures that deliver outstanding results regardless of sector. This is a book ultimately about high performance, and as I read it I found myself reflecting on some time I spent on a training course with the Red Arrows. How do you create and maintain a world-beating team capable of wing-tip-to-wing-tip stunts at several hundred miles an hour? You focus absolutely on techniques and methods that help both the individual and the team progress.

What I've learned over the years is that before systems, technology or investment comes people. Some great results come from understanding the skills and abilities of your people and applying them to the right tasks. But that is less than half the story and even less than half of the joy of leadership. The real joy comes from spotting talent and opportunity and helping that talent grow and deliver. There is nothing more satisfying than seeing people develop and progress into senior roles and working on larger projects, excelling and delivering great results in ways that you hadn't envisaged – because you took the time to help them learn and unleash their potential.

Seeing individuals progress is brilliant, but what if you could apply that same thinking and energy to whole teams, departments or businesses? What if you could apply the learning imperative to the culture of your organisation? What would results be like if everyone were on that powerful journey of development? In this book Mark and Andy provide the tools and methodology to help you cultivate in your organisation a positive learning culture which will be invaluable to anyone – not only to those who want to succeed today but also to those who want to create an organisation that can succeed regardless of the social, technological or political changes that will impact them in the future.

Matt Forrest, Executive Director of Business Development, Home Group

Acknowledgements

Mark Burns: Heartfelt thanks to my wife Kerry for your endless patience and support throughout the planning and writing of this book. To Gracie and Ruby for being wonderful distractions. Thanks also to the countless passionate individuals, dedicated to developing learning organisations, who gave their time generously to discuss ideas. Particular mention to Stuart, James, Toby, Matt, Marie, Rob, Bernie, Annie, Sean, Catherine, Michael, Roy and my sister, Sarah. To Nick, who has been a valuable source of feedback. Finally, thanks to my parents for all you have done for me over the years.

Andy Griffith: My thanks, for supporting me with research, advice and the opportunity to learn from them and their organisations, to Andy O'Brien, Carel Buxton, Caroline Saxelby, Mark Nevin, Sean Cushion, Tony McGuinness, Vincent Charnley, John Baker, Samantha McQuillan, Paul Matthews, Peter Hyman and Ian Clarke. Thanks also to my family, Clair, Joe and Anna, for their encouragement.

Contents

Introduction

This is a book about creating high quality learning in organisations – learning that leads to improved performance, motivation and personal growth. The idea for a book on this topic had been germinating within us for some time, but it was a chance conversation during a morning coffee break that spurred us into action. We were working with a group of middle managers. They were a passionate group, but they were really struggling because of the way their organisation was performing.

Over a coffee, one of the group leaned forward and whispered, 'Is everywhere else as tough as this place? I mean, how can any organisation thrive with the constant change and ever-increasing pressure we're dealing with?'

We paused to consider a response. On the one hand, it was appropriate to recognise the external pressures they were enduring. On the other hand, we had been working with two other organisations in very similar contexts during the previous fortnight which, despite the pressure, really could be described as thriving. It was the hesitation and our facial expressions that gave us away. 'No way! So what are they doing so differently? I thought it would be the same everywhere.'

This book seeks to answer the question, 'What are they doing differently?', for anyone who has ever wondered whether there is a better way.

For the last ten years, we have both worked intensively with many organisations, both in the UK and abroad. Our primary role has been to design high quality learning for employees in order to yield improved performance. At the outset, much of this work involved working directly with employees. However, over time, we have increasingly been working with leaders to help them create more impactful learning for their own teams.

Through this work, we have gained many insights into why some organisations thrive while others don't. We have been able to observe learning in organisations up close. We have analysed the key ingredients that ensure effective learning, as well as the barriers that inhibit it.

In addition, it has brought us into contact with passionate leaders who have shared with us the practical challenges they have faced when improving learning performance in their teams. As part of our research, we have interviewed many of those who have most impressed us with the way they have gone about enhancing the quality of organisational learning. From these interviews, we have been able to gather together a range of case studies and examples to bring this work to life.

We are acutely aware of the intense pressures that leaders of modern day organisations face. This appears to be a common thread across the public, private and third sectors. Consequently, in order to give you a clear, concise and, above all, practical manual, we have sought to keep the theory and academic references to a minimum. For those who would like to explore further, there are pointers to further reading at the end of each chapter.

How to use the book

We have designed the book in three sections to provide a step-by-step guide to developing high impact learning for any team.

Part I

Chapter 1 sets out *why* creating and maintaining a learning team needs to be a high priority on every leader's agenda. It is designed to help you understand why learning is central to the long-term success of any team or organisation.

Chapter 2 explores the first steps in *how* to achieve this. It provides an easy-to-use framework to help you establish exactly where your team are starting from, and the learning destination they need to get to – that is, open to learning and high performing. Using this framework will ensure that learning is targeted on the specific development needs of each individual in the team.

Part II

The chapters in Part II are designed to help you build or maintain an open-to-learning mindset in your team. This is achieved by establishing three key foundations: processing capacity for learning, strong relational trust and accurate self-perception. These foundations facilitate the development of team members who are habitually reflective, curious and open to feedback. To assist with this process, the book offers tools to diagnose any closed-to-learning mindsets and provides strategies designed to make sure that teams develop a positive learning culture.

Part III

The final part of the book provides a step-by-step guide to designing and leading effective learning for others. Whether you are planning a one-hour training session or a much longer multi-session programme, the chapters in this section will help to ensure that the learning programmes your team participate in are engaging, appropriately challenging and, most importantly, develop their performance.

Whether you are an experienced leader or someone just starting out in the role, we are confident that this intentionally practical and hands-on book will provide you with ideas and inspiration to help improve the engagement of your team and make a powerful impact on their learning. This is learning that not only supports the ongoing development of your team to meet the needs of tomorrow, but also makes each and every colleague feel valued and nurtured. That is exactly what we mean by the *learning imperative*.

Part I

Learning and your team

Chapter 1

The importance of learning

We were on the 11.07 out of Liverpool Street station. Sitting across the table from me (Mark) and my 6-year-old daughter, Ruby, was the store manager of (according to the documents in front of her) a major high street retail chain. She was making a series of calls, and, judging by the nature of the conversations, it seemed she was returning from a major review at head office. With each successive call we could sense her palpably growing frustration with various colleagues and their failure – in her eyes – to do their jobs properly.

Ruby – who, due to her curiosity, might well end up working for the secret services one day – was intrigued to eavesdrop on these conversations and was fascinated by the new range of language she was hearing. Arriving into Ipswich station, the preoccupied manager was surprised to discover that she had reached her destination. She leapt up, grabbed her belongings and hustled down the carriage. My little co-traveller observed all of this in silence. Then she turned to me and fixed me with a puzzled look. I knew a question was coming.

'Why doesn't she just teach them?'

'To do what?' I replied.

'To learn how to do their jobs properly. Then she can be less angry!'

There certainly appeared to be learning gaps in the store manager's organisation. But for whom?

■ Have you ever wondered why it is a struggle to engage your team in learning?

- Do you sometimes feel tired or stressed by constantly finding and fixing issues in your team?

- Do you find 'developing your team' the one task on your to-do list that you never get to?

What's in this chapter for me?

This chapter will examine first why learning is such a crucial foundation to the future success of all teams and organisations. Having addressed the imperative of learning, we will then go on to explore the common reasons why learning is not always given the priority it deserves. As part of this process, we will give you the opportunity to reflect on your own team or organisation and the importance of its ongoing growth and development.

What do we mean by a 'learning team'?

A team, as we define it in this book, is the particular group of people who you directly lead or over whom you have direct or indirect influence. This could be a small team of two or three or, if you are a chief executive, a team of several hundred to many thousands.

As the authors of this book, we are making the assumption that you, the reader, are curious about the value of learning for your team and organisation, and seeking clarity and practical strategies to help develop and implement effective and sustainable learning and development.

Throughout the book, we will use case studies from real life. We will cite the experiences of individuals, teams and organisations we have worked with to illustrate the principles and strategies we are advocating. Our case studies are drawn from a wide range of contexts, locations and types of organisation. They include those that have learning and development deeply embedded in their DNA, and those that don't. We will also include the learning journeys of organisations and leaders who thought they were optimising the learning of their staff, but who later came to realise that the approaches they were using were ineffective.

Drawing on our experiences, we suggest that a learning team is a group of individuals who commit to learn together. After all, down the ages, human development has been enhanced by people collaborating, sharing learning and struggling through adversity to explore new ideas, new perspectives, new possibilities. We consider how this collaborative power can be focused on ensuring the ongoing growth and development of your team and your organisation into the future.

In what contexts does learning take place?

Learning takes place in many forms in organisations. On some occasions it will be through formal learning programmes. More often, however, it will be in less formal situations such as on-the-job experiences. In this setting, individuals learn from their mistakes as they attempt to master their work role and from the feedback they receive on their performance. Individuals also learn alongside fellow workers through a variety of activities, including social learning, coaching, mentoring, collaborative learning and other methods of engagement with peers. This book will help you to maximise the potential for learning across each of these contexts.

Learning can take many different forms. One of the models we have found most useful in achieving deep learning is the KASH model. This stands for the ongoing development of the *knowledge*, *attitudes*, *skills* and *habits* of individuals within teams and which contributes to individual and collective improved performance. While Paul Kirschner, John Sweller and Richard Clark have defined learning as 'a change in long-term memory',[1] in the workplace, learning is likely to lead to the acquisition of knowledge, attitudes, skills and habits which are readily available from memory to use.

The pursuit of KASH reminds us that this book isn't just about how to design effective learning in our team, although we cover that in Part III. This book explores much, much more. One of our key aims is to support you to foster an

---

1   Paul A. Kirschner, John Sweller and Richard E. Clark, 'Why Minimal Guidance During Instruction Does Not Work: An Analysis of the Failure of Constructivist, Discovery, Problem-Based, Experiential, and Inquiry-Based Teaching', *Educational Psychologist*, 41(2) (2006), 75–86 at 75.

environment in which a strong learning team, who are intrinsically motivated to grow and develop, can thrive.

Knowledge	Attitudes
Skills	Habits

You can download a free KASH template at: www.learningimperative.co.uk/downloads/KASH.

Why is a learning team an 'imperative' rather than a 'nice to have'?

As one leader said to us, as we sat with him in his office reflecting on three tumultuous years of change, 'Guys, it's been an interesting three years. However, we're looking forward now to calmer waters while we embed the changes we have made.' Just two weeks later we received an email from him. 'Spoke too soon,' it said. 'Just had confirmation of a three-year programme of budget cuts from HQ. It'll be 10% off our budget. We're back in the world of change again.'

Whether in the public, private or third sector, organisations are experiencing more change than ever before.[2] Whether this is driven by technological advances, the effects of increasing globalisation, the after-effects of the financial crash or changing population demographics, it has meant that calm waters are a dim and distant memory for many.

In parallel with internal drivers for change, organisations are driven by consumers (whether paying customers or not) demanding greater choice. When we were young men in the 1970s, choice was much more restricted. Research in the United States found that in the 1970s the average supermarket stocked 9,000 different items. Nowadays that number is nearer 40,000.[3] If you don't believe us, take a walk down the breakfast cereal aisle in your local supermarket – it is about 20 metres long!

This abundance of choice for consumers places enormous pressures on organisations. Not just consumer choice about what to buy but, given the growth of the internet, greater choice in how to purchase products and access services. All sectors continue to pursue more effective ways to connect with their customers, better meet their needs and have a more positive impact on the end-users of the product or service – and, as a consequence, improve sales and profits or surpluses.

Now, more than ever before, there is a compelling need for organisations to develop learning teams who have the agility to adapt. After all, if we are not open to learning from these changes, and the opportunities and threats they present, what hope does our team or organisation have of surviving in these turbulent times, let alone thriving?

---

2   See Jenny Roper, 'Organisations Must Prepare for Rapid Pace of Change', *HR Magazine* (11 March 2016). Available at: http://hrmagazine.co.uk/article-details/organisations-must-prepare-for-rapid-pace-of-change.
3   See Daniel Levitin, *The Organized Mind: Thinking Straight in the Age of Information Overload* (New York: Penguin, 2015), p. 5.

Reflection questions

What have been the main changes in your industry in the last five years?

Do you agree that change is getting faster in your industry?

How has the pace of change affected you and your team?

What have been the main changes in your organisation in the last five years?

How have these changes affected what your team does and how your team works?

What job roles have disappeared or changed?

Improving the quality of what you do

In recent years, the buzz phrase 'marginal gains' has achieved legendary status.[4] It is an approach that certain teams in sport and industry have adopted as they seek to develop learning cultures which are relentlessly focused on improving quality and performance. The phrase is prominent in the media, and it is creeping more and more into presentations given by leaders to their teams.

But this philosophy has been alive and well since the 1950s, when Japanese car manufacturer Toyota developed its celebrated approach to learning-centred improvement.[5] This process led to them creating an unrivalled reputation for producing the highest quality cars with fewer defects than any of their competitors'. Indeed, the approach was so influential that not only did other car

---

4   See Matthew Syed, *Black Box Thinking: The Surprising Truth About Success* (London: John Murray, 2015).

5   See Jeffrey K. Liker, *The Toyota Way: 14 Management Principles from the World's Greatest Manufacturer* (Columbus, OH: McGraw-Hill Education, 2004).

manufacturers adopt similar strategies, but so did firms in a wide range of other fields.

Toyota's approach to learning embodies two key principles – *kaizen* (continuous improvement) and *hansei* (relentless reflection). *Kaizen* is underpinned by Toyota's 'five whys' analysis. Asking why five times when any problem arises enables a team to methodically surface the deeper, systemic causes of a problem and therefore reach more effective solutions. In this approach, 'errors are seen as opportunities for learning' and 'Learning is a continuous company-wide process'[6]. In his groundbreaking work on systems thinking, Peter Senge noted that with this method 'people continually expand their capacity to create results'.[7] Senge's work invites us to pose an important question: unless a strong habit of learning is embedded in our teams, how can you possibly ensure a rich, ongoing dialogue about ways to improve the quality of our organisation's services or products?

The footnote to Toyota's phenomenal worldwide growth over fifty years reinforces the imperative of learning. At the end of the 2000s, Toyota ran into a spectacular and very costly furore surrounding the safety of more than 1.66 million of their cars in the United States. The negative publicity they received was exacerbated by their slow initial response. The company president, Akio Toyoda, later admitted that Toyota had prioritised growth over the maintenance of the company's culture.[8] It led to a renewed internal focus on getting back to the basics of the Toyota way, as well as analysing and implementing the learning from the setbacks.

Improved quality is key in an era of greater competition and change. It is fundamental both for ensuring that existing customers remain loyal and for attracting new customers.

---

6 Liker, *The Toyota Way*, p. 250.
7 Peter Senge, *The Fifth Discipline: The Art and Practice of the Learning Organization* (London and Boston, MA: Nicholas Brealey, 1990), p. 3.
8 See Angela Greiling Keane and Makiko Kitamura, 'Toyota Credibility Gap on Recalls Sunk in After President's Visit to US', *Bloomberg News* (10 May 2010).

Belief in growth and development for all

It is not just the quality of what the team creates that is important. Many of the leaders we interviewed pointed to other long-term outcomes they valued. One of them was a head teacher close to retirement. Asked what her greatest legacy was, she surprised us by not focusing on the succession of schools that had been transformed under her leadership. Instead, she listed a stream of former staff who had gone on to be successful leaders elsewhere, instilling the same ethos of learning within their own teams: 'It's my contribution to growing a "learning movement" amongst school leaders that I'm most proud of.'

Motivation theorists including Abraham Maslow[9] and Frederick Herzberg[10] point to the individual importance of being valued and having opportunities for personal growth and development. Jack Zenger and Joseph Folkman found in their research that 'Developing others has the twofold impact of elevating performance and creating a culture that is fun and engaging. It also attracts more people who want to work in it.'[11]

Unless a culture of learning is embedded in your teams, how can you be sure that you are motivating and engaging them effectively?

Motivation 'cement'

It is the team's learning process, as much as its output, which contributes to its effectiveness. One leader we interviewed described learning as 'the cement that bonds my team together, making it more cohesive and resilient'. What he was getting at is the power of human connectivity that can develop as part of an effective learning process.

---

9   Abraham H. Maslow, 'A Theory of Human Motivation', *Psychological Review*, 50(4) (1943), 370–396.

10 Frederick Herzberg, Bernard Mausner and Barbara Bloch Snyderman, *Motivation to Work* (London and New Brunswick, NJ: Transaction Publishers, 2011).

11 Jack Zenger and Joseph Folkman, 'How Managers Drive Results and Employee Engagement at the Same Time', *Harvard Business Review* (19 June 2017). Available at: https://hbr.org/2017/06/how-managers-drive-results-and-employee-engagement-at-the-same-time.

Learning is not always easy. It can sometimes leave learners in situations where they encounter setbacks or get 'stuck'. In work we have done developing teacher quality in schools, we have often found that it is much harder for teachers to improve their performance when they work in isolation. In addition, they also find it more difficult to sustain any improvement.

Similarly, our work with sports coaches confirms that learning seems to be much more effective when it is a collaborative, social activity. This may well be because learning alongside others provides natural opportunities for communication and dialogue. Some of this dialogue will be focused on providing moral support for each other when the learning journey becomes a struggle. However, it is the fact that dialogue creates new shared meaning that is most powerful. Such dialogue may take the form of questions, stories or examples, and helps the collaborative learner to make sense of the new learning. At the same time, dialogue provides valuable feedback to each member of the group about how to improve and move forward.

An invaluable, if indirect, consequence of a learning culture is that the human desire for meaningful social interaction is met, and this helps many individuals to feel more valued. For some staff this is an incredibly important part of what motivates them. One leader we interviewed commented, 'Since my organisation has embraced learning, I see and hear a more sociable team. People genuinely want to spend time with each other. One colleague told me that they look forward to Monday mornings more, as they sense they are "working with like minds".'

Nurturing curiosity

Sitting in on a team meeting one Tuesday afternoon, we were struck by what was taking place. Each of the team was taking their turn in the 'hot seat'. The occupant of the hot seat would provide the rest of the team with an update on progress in his or her own area of responsibility. Everyone else, including the team leader, acted as interrogators, enquiring and probing with questions. This challenged the hot seat's occupant to explain their thinking with greater care and consider the quality of their future planning more deeply.

No quarter was given or taken, yet despite the challenging nature of the exercise it was clear that the strong relationships within the team were unaffected. After the session, the team leader told us that this curious and demanding learning community was not something he had inherited when he took on the role: 'No, I had to work hard to get them to realise that the whole point of meetings is to test and challenge our existing thinking in order to consider other viewpoints and perspectives. Meetings are not for sitting in silence. They have definitely got the benefit of this now. As a group of learners we consistently make better decisions because we are more curious and more demanding.'

Later in the book, we will explore tools that can transform your meetings from pedestrian information dumps to more highly tuned opportunities to develop new directions and possibilities using creative methods such as 'pre-mortems' which build a more open-to-learning culture.

We're committed to learning, aren't we?

Surely, every leader wants their team to be engaged in improving what they do, wants them to consistently develop higher levels of performance, wants them to be better equipped to face future uncertainty, wants them to provide better quality outputs that reduce the need for difficult conversations about underperformance? The learning imperative is unquestionably a compelling call.

Well, yes and no. Many leaders we have worked with do indeed put the learning and development of their team at the heart of what they say and do. The imperative runs through them like the letters in a stick of seaside rock. When we shadow these leaders, learning can be seen happening on a day-to-day basis, not only in themselves but also in their teams, even when they are working independently of their leader. Learning has become habitual and widespread in these organisations.

There is another group of leaders we have worked with for whom learning and development is not valued as an imperative. In fact, learning is not on their radar. From our observations and from listening to hundreds of individuals and teams, we have found that this is normally due to one of five causes.

As you read about each of these factors, we encourage you to honestly rate yourself on a scale of 'completely me' to 'not me at all'.

1. I haven't got time for this

There are some leaders who take the view that learning is something they will get around to once they have dealt with the short-term concerns they are facing. Issues persist over time, and before we know it, short term has become medium term and medium term becomes long term. One leader we worked with typified this kind of procrastination. In our first session with him, he had come to the conclusion that he needed to develop the quality of learning in his team. He said, 'It's the only game in town for us. I promise it'll happen.' But when we met up again some months later, he had the demeanour of a slimmer turning up to a Weight Watchers meeting after a week of bingeing. 'I know, I know,' he blustered. 'I know I said I'd change, but we've just been sooo busy!'

Of course, time is a legitimate constraint. However, a great deal of time is often invested in micro-managing staff who are underperforming due to lack of training. Instead of steadily developing the internal capacity of their teams to become more skilled and higher performing, micro-managers micro-manage quality issues on a day-to-day basis. As a result, the performance of teams where micro-management is the norm, despite the Herculean caffeine-fuelled efforts of their managers, is inferior to those teams in which staff are fully engaged in the ongoing learning process. Micro-managed teams suffer from lower staff morale, too.

The adrenaline rush that comes with unilateral, power-in-action management can appear more seductive than collaboratively nurturing the slower, more incremental development of a learning team. But wisdom and experience would suggest that we heed the old adage: 'Give me six hours to chop down a tree and I'll spend the first four sharpening my axe.'

Completely me   Sometimes me   Not me at all

Reflection questions

Do find yourself spending too much time dealing with problems that have arisen because individuals in your team are underperforming?

Do you ever avoid delegation because you lack confidence in members of your team to do the job?

What would your day be like if you didn't have to micro-manage, since your team had developed the capacity to learn and take greater ownership?

2. Treating the effects, not addressing the causes

Somewhat related to the perception of lack of time and micro-management, the second blind spot is the compulsion to focus on the effects rather than the causes of problems. A couple of years ago, we were working with a group of relatively inexperienced middle leaders in London. We asked them to work in small groups and analyse the knotty issues they were facing when leading their teams – the sort of problem, like having a stone in your shoe, that was giving them cause for discomfort. Having asked them to identify the effects of these difficulties, we then invited them to evaluate the likely causes. It didn't take long for them to make some important connections. 'I get it,' said Imran. 'I have to switch my attention to dealing with the causes.'

As educator Michael Fullan puts it, 'There is more to accountability than measuring results; you need to develop people's capacity to achieve the results.'[12] Imran realised that he had been too busy holding individuals in his team to account and offering nothing more than remedial action. Instead, he saw that he needed to

---

12 Michael Fullan, *The Principal: Three Keys to Maximizing Impact* (San Francisco, CA: Jossey-Bass, 2014), p. 27.

focus his energies on creating effective learning opportunities for his team so they could improve their performance in the long term.

Completely me   Sometimes me   Not me at all

Reflection questions

What are the 'stones in the shoe' problems that exist in your team?

To what extent do you find yourself dealing with the effects rather than the causes of problems?

3. Things seem OK-ish as they are right now

Naz is an uber-impressive leader whose relentless, energetic focus on learning has led her to develop numerous other leaders in her industry. She has a great aversion to what she calls 'the curse of OK'. Whenever she senses that 'OK thinking' is setting in, she embarks on an energised call to arms with her team. One such passionate eruption that we observed started off like this: 'I didn't get out of bed today to have an "OK" day, or an "OK" meeting, or just "OK" relations with my team. I don't want "Naz was OK" on my gravestone!' She knows the risks that the inertia and mediocrity of OK thinking brings. She doesn't want it infecting her team. It is the reason why each year she ratchets up a couple more notches what passes as 'high quality' within her team.

Ultimately, very few leaders are prepared to settle for OK, but when tired and stressed the comfort blanket that comes with thinking that things seem OK can be seductive. The problem for the OK thinking team is that OK might lead to KO (knock out) at some point in the future. This could be due to the relentless pace of change, being overtaken by more ambitious competitors or, as is so often the case when a culture of OK-ness prevails, learning within the team stops and individuals begin to slip into unthinking habits, just going through the motions. 'What we've always done has been OK,' they say, 'I'll just keep doing what I'm doing.' OK thinking can reduce visibility to the need for change or to the problems occurring right under our noses.

Completely me   Sometimes me   Not me at all

Reflection questions

How often do you reach for the comfort blanket labelled 'things are OK'?

To what extent does OK thinking affect your team?

4. If we train them, they will leave

In an era of low unemployment and skills shortages, there is a theoretical risk that investing time and money in developing high quality learning will lead to individuals leaving the organisation. They may be poached or simply feel better equipped to find a new job with higher status or pay. Who wants to be a free training resource for other organisations?

There is a paradox here though. This isn't a zero-sum game – there are plenty of downsides to not investing in learning. This was abundantly clear in a meeting we attended some years ago. One manager argued passionately against investing in learning and development for the reasons just mentioned. His final point was, 'What happens if we train them and they leave? It's just time and money wasted.' To which, after a pause, a colleague drily responded, 'What happens if we don't and they stay?'

It may be the case that individuals in your team – individuals you have developed – will leave. However, unless you are managing the 'lifers' wing of a prison, many individuals will decide to move on at some point anyway. Our argument, based on our experience and the research cited earlier (see page 14), is that individuals will stay for longer in teams in which they feel valued, where they are being developed and where they have a deep sense of engagement through the tangible impact they are making. A big part of this engagement comes from learning being at the heart of everything they do.

Completely me   Sometimes me   Not me at all

Reflection questions

To what extent does the fear of individuals leaving create an unwillingness to develop learning in your team?

How far do the benefits of not investing in learning outweigh the costs?

5. Leopards can't change their spots

This final cause runs deep in some leaders: they are simply closed to learning. Their belief is that there are individuals in their team who are not capable of learning and developing to the required level.

One leader we worked with finally saw the light. She reflected ruefully, 'I've come to the painful conclusion that my organisation can't move forward under my leadership until I change my mindset. Right now, it's my belief that they're incapable of learning – that's the core of the problem.' She had discovered the power of self-fulfilling prophecy: the more we think negatively, the more chance there is of creating a negative outcome. For this leader, the honest self-appraisal was the most important first step for her and her organisation in turning the corner and moving forward.

What makes this negative mindset so destructive is that it can unintentionally infect our thoughts and interactions with our team. It can be an unconscious bias that affects everything we do and think. As the old saying goes, 'We do not see things as they are, we see things as we are.' Why do some leaders lapse into this negative cycle of thinking? In Part II, we will explore some of the factors that lead some people into limiting beliefs about what others can do. In our experience, individuals and teams are capable of achieving a great deal more than others might expect.

Completely me   Sometimes me   Not me at all

Reflection questions

To what extent do you have a negative, closed-to-learning belief about individuals in your team? If you do, how does it show up in your thoughts and actions?

How do you think those beliefs might have been formed?

Conclusion

As leaders, we have to decide whether to invest time, effort and reputational risk in developing learning in our teams. However, we also need to be aware of the consequences of not making that choice. Choosing to do nothing may lead to fewer opportunities for personal and professional development within our teams. It could also mean rejecting possibilities to learn about learning and the many advantages this brings socially and organisationally. Whichever way we choose will have an impact on our teams, our organisations and ourselves.

Peter Block, in his wonderful book *Community*, asks us to consider whether we are part of a 'community of possibilities' or a 'community of problems'.[13] It is the community of possibilities that has the capacity to increase its impact beyond the current situation and towards a desired future. This may well include a better version of our current team. But if we lack the recognition of the possibilities that a learning culture provides, then we are likely to find ourselves stuck with our current problems without the capacity or agility to overcome them.

Imagine for a moment that at your retirement all the people you have ever worked with gathered to talk about what you did for them. They haven't come to

13 Peter Block, *Community: The Structure of Belonging* (San Francisco, CA: Berrett-Koehler, 2009), p. 30.

boost your ego, but to reflect on how working alongside you impacted on their personal and professional lives. What would you want them to say?

Reflection questions

What would be the benefits to you, your team and your organisation of a strong learning culture?

What will be the impact on your customers, and their experience of working with your team, as a result of a strong learning culture?

Do the benefits outweigh the costs of investing time in learning?

What are the risks of ignoring learning for your team's future success?

REFRESH reading list

In the next chapter we will deconstruct the characteristics of effective learners by using our model, REFRESH. Here is some suggested reading if you want to deepen your own learning about aspects of this first chapter:

Block, Peter (2009). *Community: The Structure of Belonging* (San Francisco, CA: Berrett-Koehler).

Johnson, Whitney (2018). *Build an A-Team: Play to Their Strengths and Lead Them Up the Learning Curve* (Boston, MA: Harvard Business Review Press).

Kline, Nancy (1999). *Time to Think: Listening to Ignite the Human Mind* (London: Cassell Illustrated).

Liker, Jeffrey K. (2004). *The Toyota Way: 14 Management Principles from the World's Greatest Manufacturer* (Columbus, OH: McGraw Hill Education).

Staats, Bradley R. (2018). *Never Stop Learning: Stay Relevant, Reinvent Yourself and Thrive* (Boston, MA: Harvard Business Review Press).

Chapter 2

The learning–performance matrix

'Would you tell me, please, which way I ought to go from here?'

'That depends a good deal on where you want to get to,' said the Cat.

'I don't much care where –' said Alice.

'Then it doesn't matter which way you go,' said the Cat.

'– so long as I get SOMEWHERE,' Alice added as an explanation.

'Oh, you're sure to do that,' said the Cat, 'if you only walk long enough.'

Lewis Carroll, *Alice's Adventures in Wonderland*[1]

What's in this chapter for me?

This chapter will provide you with clear guidance on how to define the learning destination for your team and the level that you would like your team to be working at consistently. Once this first stage has been defined, we will show you how

1   Lewis Carroll, *Alice's Adventures in Wonderland* (London: Penguin Random House, 2015 [1896]), p. 27.

to establish the starting points for your individual team members. This valuable process, once completed, will unlock your ability to map out exactly how to design the learning journey for your team using Parts II and III of the book.

- Have you ever felt like Alice, slightly perplexed in terms of which direction to take to develop your team?

- Have you ever had experiences in the past where efforts to develop learning in your team have resulted in patchy impact?

- Have you been convinced of the imperative to grow a learning team but aren't sure where to start?

What are the potential effects of poorly designed learning?

About six years ago we were contacted by an organisation in some difficulty. The manager wanted our support, but he had set his heart on a specific plan that he wanted us to help him implement. He had seen this strategy work in a different organisation sometime before; however, the problem was that his current organisation was starting from a very different place. Like a novice golfer selecting the wrong club in the sand trap, it was a plan that was doomed to failure.

The mantra 'the customer is always right' was running through our minds as we listened to him talk enthusiastically. He had in mind a peer coaching programme – the sort of programme that can work effectively, but with two important conditions: first, the culture of the team has to be right and, second, team members need to be skilled in coaching and being coached. Unfortunately, neither condition was present. Consequently, it was destined to fail unless we could help him see the gaps in his plan.

Taking swift action to design a learning programme can give the illusion that things will improve. However, when learning is not thought through and is poorly designed, there can be two unfortunate consequences. First, there is the measurable expense of the time and money that will be invested in the project. This financial outlay can often be underestimated because, in addition to the visible costs of engaging external consultants and providing a training venue and refreshments, there are also the invisible costs of the salaries of the team taking part in the training. Time out of the office is an expense. If the team is large and/ or the training programme is significant in duration, this can be a much bigger cost than that accounted for on the invoices of the trainers and venue providers.

Much more damaging in the long term, though, can be the qualitative costs – in particular, the team's negative perception of the value of learning interventions. If a team have experienced poor quality, ill-planned learning, they can develop a pervasive negative response to new learning opportunities, regardless of their quality. Furthermore, ineffective learning programmes can damage the reputation of the leader who has placed great store in them. This can sometimes be more detrimental than the financial costs because it creates resistance to any future learning programmes.

Case study: initiative overload

Some years ago at a conference in London, I (Andy) was waiting to lead a session for more than 150 people. The leader of the organisation opened the day by giving a keynote address. It seemed energising stuff as he linked what I was going to speak about to his big vision. I was sitting at the back of the auditorium among some of the least enthusiastic employees, one of whom turned to his neighbour and whispered, 'He'll have forgotten all this within three months and be chasing something else shiny.'

In this chapter we will introduce you to our learning–performance matrix. This is designed to help you establish the most appropriate starting points for your team's high impact learning, specifically customised to their particular needs. It will also help you to avoid the two ever-present dangers listed above: wasting valuable resources and inadvertently developing resistance to learning.

Ready, aim, fire: the importance of building a coherent plan for learning

Given the clear risks of poorly designed learning, which we outlined above, our aim is to provide a clear step-by-step process to develop a well-thought-out plan of action. This process will enable you to sieve through the vast array of strategies available in order to select the most appropriate for your context. 'By all means,' we say to leaders, 'you are welcome to ignore the research and evidence that suggests your plan is doomed to failure. However, please do so with your eyes wide open to the potential consequences.'

In order to develop a credible plan, it is crucially important to work through two steps. The first step is to identify clearly what 'high performance' would look, sound and feel like for your team. There is a danger of embarking on actions without a clear direction or focus if the desired destination is not clearly established. Once the destination is ascertained, it becomes much easier to evaluate whether progress is moving in the right direction against the set criteria. This is evidence-based learning: are the behaviours, relationships and attitudes within the team moving towards what you have agreed that you want to see, hear and feel?

Once the desired outcome has been established, the second step requires you to accurately assess the starting points of each individual member of your team. Our experience over the last ten years informs us that, unless these two steps are carefully worked through, effective learning is rarely possible.

Where are we now?

Whenever we have worked with leaders who have found themselves stuck when trying to improve the impact of learning in their teams, we use the learning–performance matrix (see page 29). It helps them to map out the learners' start points and the desired destination. The matrix acts as a brake. By slowing down, leaders are less likely to fall into the seductive, but often counter-productive, pitfall of ready, fire, aim – too hastily embarking on actions that are based on neither evidence nor research.

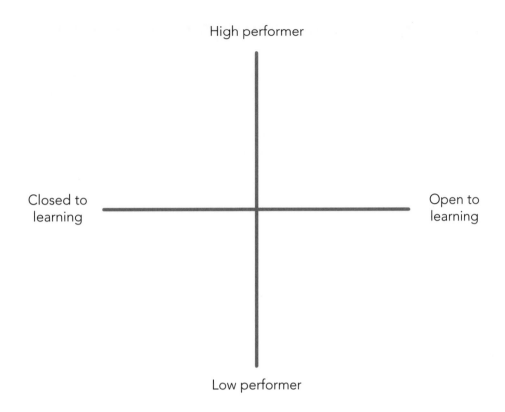

The vertical axis of the matrix plots the individual against a high performer–low performer continuum. The horizontal axis is a continuum representing whether the individual is closed to learning or open to learning. We will discuss each axis in detail so you can decide where to plot the starting points of each individual in your team.

The high performer–low performer continuum

The first stage in the process is to isolate the vertical axis and really get to grips with a detailed understanding of what high performance means in your team.

High
performer

Low
performer

The high performer is any person in your team who demonstrates a level of quality that puts a smile on your face and does the same for your customers. They make you proud to work with them. Importantly, they are people who are great at what they do on a consistent, day-to-day basis. If you are lucky, you may already have one or more of these people in your team. Or you might have none. Often, though, different individuals will have some of the characteristics but not others. There may also be people who used to work in the team that others still remember as excellent models.

Defining the characteristics of the high performer accurately is crucially important for three reasons:

1   Unless there is absolute clarity about what high performer means, there will be no clear benchmarks against which to accurately measure each individual in the team. It is essential to start any training with a clear notion of the gap between current performance and the desired standard.

2   If certain high performer characteristics are overlooked or omitted at this stage, then they inevitably won't be a focus for learning/development, even though some individuals in the team may lack them. Ensure that all key criteria are included.

3   Feedback and dialogue play a crucial role in helping to improve performance. However, the effectiveness of feedback depends on shared clarity about what you mean by high performer. If this is ill defined, the effectiveness of feedback will be diminished.

Case study: defining high performance

A major high street store invited us to help them redesign their training programme for new store staff. It is a programme that is now running successfully across their UK and Ireland stores. The first stage in the process was to get the learning and development team to sit down and define what exactly was a high performing sales assistant. Sometimes this question can provoke looks of, 'Well, isn't it obvious?' – but not with this group of passionate individuals. Instead, an earnest debate developed as the deconstruction process unfolded. These valuable discussions led to a shared clarity about what they meant by a high performer in their stores. They later reflected on just how important it had been to agree these criteria up front, so that all the key aspects they needed to develop in their new staff were covered.

We use the KASH model to help define the ingredients for a high performer. As we saw in Chapter 1, KASH stands for knowledge, attitudes, skills and habits. This model enables leaders to deconstruct and tightly define the different attributes of the high performer.

Using KASH to deconstruct the qualities of a high performer can be a more challenging task than it initially seems. Much of what makes the high performer so effective may actually be invisible and inaudible. It may well be part of a person's thinking process that ensures he or she does their job so well. For example, in the case study above, one aspect of the KASH of high performing sales assistants was their skill in noticing which customers needed help or advice. They would regularly scan the shop floor looking for such customers rather than getting completely engrossed in another task, such as stock replenishment.

It is also possible to suffer from the 'curse of the expert' blind spot.[2] This occurs when a skill or behaviour becomes so second nature or intuitive that it is no longer noticed. The more we carry out a task, the more habitual it can become, and we gradually become unconsciously competent.[3] Deconstructing KASH requires us to make our unconscious competence conscious so that no key elements are missed.

Some team leaders fall into the quagmire of debating the finer differences between knowledge and skills and skills and habits![4] In our experience, this is completely unproductive. Our advice is to focus on the process of deconstructing the high performer fully. The classification of the characteristics is less important at this stage. The most important thing is to ensure that you have fully mapped out what high performing means.

---

2   See Sian Beilock, 'The Curse of Expertise', *Psychology Today* (23 March 2011). Available at: https://www.psychologytoday.com/gb/blog/choke/201103/the-curse-expertise.

3   See Linda Adams, 'Learning a New Skill is Easier Said Than Done', *Gordon Training International* (n.d.). Available at: http://www.gordontraining.com/free-workplace-articles/learning-a-new-skill-is-easier-said-than-done/.

4   Anders Ericsson and Robert Pool, in their highly influential book *Peak: How All of Us Can Achieve Extraordinary Things* (New York: Vintage Books, 2017), prefer to describe performance as it encapsulates both skill *and* knowledge.

Reflection questions

What knowledge would a high performer in your team need to have?

What attitudes would a high performer in your team need to demonstrate?

What skills would a high performer in your team be proficient in?

What habits and routines would a high performer in your team have?

What would working in your team look, sound and feel like if it was populated by colleagues with this KASH?

Case study: KASH deconstruction

As an example of how one organisation defined the KASH for a high performer, we worked with the inspirational charity It's Your Life, based in Tower Hamlets, London. The charity was seeking to develop an effective training programme to enable their high impact parenting programme, It's Your Child's Life, to succeed in Liverpool.

Sitting down with the CEO, Jackie Barnes, we created a plan to enable her to deconstruct the KASH of a high performing programme leader. This involved surfacing the competencies which she herself had nurtured during her development of the programme. She videoed herself leading sessions so that she could evaluate how she led the programme. In addition, she observed her training team running similar sessions so she could analyse all the key elements of high performance.

Knowledge	Attitudes
■ Course content and processes	■ Belief that all parents can improve
■ Knowledge of how to get buy-in from parents	■ Desire to make a real and lasting difference to the lives of families and children
■ Practical tools and strategies parents can use	■ Resilient
■ Understanding of key barriers to change	■ Curious
■ Knowledge of each family's context	■ Non-judgemental
■ Knowledge of parents' context (e.g. health issues)	■ Open to learning about the barriers that parents encounter and how to overcome them
■ Understanding of how humans learn	■ Open to feedback from others on how to improve
■ Knowledge of support agencies within the local area	■ Humble (so that parents don't perceive they are being told how to parent)
■ Knowledge of the range of specific learning difficulties	
■ Requirements for Early Learning goals for children	

Skills	Habits
■ Interpersonal skills	■ Personal organisation
■ Trust building with parents	■ Reflective on how to improve their own performance
■ Communication with schools/ parents/link teacher	■ Adjusting the planning and delivery of sessions to meet the individual needs of parents
■ Questioning and nurturing dialogue	

- Listening
- Coaching/mentoring
- Planning and prioritising
- Developing a 'can do' attitude among parents
- Managing and facilitating rich, open discussions
- Diagnostic in identifying the causes of issues at home

- Creating a sense of high expectations among parents

Based on this work, Jackie recruited and trained two course leaders who are now leading successful parenting programmes in primary schools across Merseyside.

 Reflection questions

Which KASH elements are most important in your team?

Which KASH elements are most commonly missing?

If you could improve one KASH element in your existing team which one would it be? What benefits would it bring to you, your team and your customers?

How does your team profile compare with the KASH of the high performer? Where is it strong? Where are the biggest gaps?

How effective have your past efforts been in developing the KASH you have identified for your team?

The open-to-learning–closed-to-learning continuum

Closed to
learning

Open to
learning

Just because a person is open to learning, it doesn't necessarily mean they are a high performer. Conversely, it is also true that while it requires learning to become a high performer, that same high performer may become closed to learning.

At the core of being open to learning is an ongoing, intrinsically driven commitment to growth and development which the learner applies to both themselves and their team. Our observations from working with open-to-learning individuals in teams is that they share the following REFRESH learning characteristics:

■ **Resilience**: open learners are resilient when learning. They demonstrate a willingness to persevere to improve their own performance and support the improvement of others. They are not easily deterred when things don't advance quickly. They recognise that learning is an iterative process during which individuals and teams use feedback to continually improve what they do.

■ **Enquiring**: open learners have an innate curiosity about why things are done in a certain way, and how they might be done differently and more effectively. They ask questions, not because they are being obstructive, but because they are keen to deepen their understanding about how the work of the team can be done effectively. They might ask: why have problems occurred? What solutions might solve these problems? Why is one solution better than another? What kind of thinking led to this particular solution being proposed in the first place? How can we ensure future problems don't arise? The positive results they achieve from their curiosity seem to further feed their openness to learning in a sort of virtuous cycle.

- **Feedback**: open learners crave feedback. It enables them to find out which learning gaps they have closed and which gaps remain. Consequently, feedback is used to help them reprioritise their next steps. Should they go back and improve an aspect of their existing performance, or push on to the next level? Seeking feedback is a habit for these individuals. They will often ask others for feedback in order to better understand the impact of what they do and how they work.

- **Revising**: a key characteristic of open learners is their willingness to evaluate new knowledge and adapt their existing mental model of the world to it. This new knowledge might challenge them to reject existing well-developed habits in favour of cultivating new skillsets. This willingness to experiment is underpinned by a constant desire to improve the impact of what they do. This desire leads them to challenge strongly held beliefs and unpick unconscious biases. For these individuals, change and adaptation is part of their mindset.

- **Effortful**: learning can be difficult at times. It requires new skills to be practised, new knowledge to be understood and retained, and new habits to be developed. Effective learners appreciate that this takes time and effort, and are willing to invest fully in the process.

- **Sharing**: effective learners seek authentic opportunities to maximise the benefits achieved from working collaboratively. While some individuals will have a preference for learning by themselves, collaboration can enhance learning by enabling sharing through dialogue, feedback and reflection. Collaborative learning can provide support and encouragement for individuals when they get stuck or encounter setbacks.

- **Habitual**: individuals who are open to learning see their work as intrinsically engaging. They view learning as an ongoing process which isn't constrained by working hours. At a recent meeting, Andy overheard a team member confess that he had come up with an innovative solution to a particularly tricky human resources problem while out on an early morning run! This is part of the way that open learners operate. It is in their DNA. Coffee breaks become research and development discussions and spontaneous Friday afternoon reflection sessions spring up without the need for a team leader to compile an agenda.

Reflection questions

Consider the most open-to-learning individual in your team. How do they demonstrate the REFRESH characteristics on a day-to-day basis? What is the impact of this openness to learning?

Which of the REFRESH characteristics are most commonly present in your team?

And which characteristics are most often missing?

What is the impact of your answers to the previous two questions?

Which of these characteristics do you find easiest to model yourself?

And which characteristics do you find more difficult?

Human ego – the brake pedal on learning

One of the characteristics that marks out really successful learners and team players is their ability and willingness to balance their own ego needs for achieving personal goals with the drive to foster collective growth and development within the team. Where this balance is lacking, or where an individual ego is immature, the idea of success is focused on personal rather than team achievement – that is, a desire to look better than others, a tendency to take feedback personally rather than as an invitation to development, and a mindset that leads these individuals to value being liked and admired above all else.

Time and again we have found that where learning has ground to a halt in teams, immature and unhealthy egos have been a major cause. When a needy ego has been allowed to dominate, whether it is that of a team member or their leader, an unhelpful or even toxic environment of distrust can easily develop. Such distrust quickly and corrosively undermines relationships and collaboration. David

Marcum and Steven Smith, in their excellent book *Egonomics*, refer to the need to ensure that there is a balance between ego and humility.[5] This equilibrium helps to ensure that feedback is viewed as developmental, not personal, and can therefore be given and received openly and honestly. The role of the ego is an aspect of team learning that will be revisited in much more detail in Part II.

Case study: the curse of 'I'

Observing a team meeting in an organisation several years ago, it quickly became apparent that one individual's needy ego and dominant personality were damaging the potential for effective learning in the team. This person repeatedly made contributions prefixed with 'I'. He was keen to share his own personal successes, to which the team responded with a great deal of eye rolling. It reminded us of the old Spanish proverb, 'Tell me what you brag about and I'll tell you what you lack.'

What are the starting points of your team?

Now that we have demystified the two axes of the learning–performance matrix, the next task is to plot the starting positions of your own team. If you are not sure about a particular individual, note down an initial position in pencil and then watch and listen intently to him or her for a couple of days. It is amazing what you notice when you know what to look and listen for!

You can download a blank copy of the learning–performance matrix at: www.learningimperative.co.uk/downloads/LP-Matrix.

---

5 David Marcum and Steven Smith, *Egonomics: What Makes Ego Our Greatest Asset (Or Most Expensive Liability)* (New York: Simon & Schuster, 2007), p. 13.

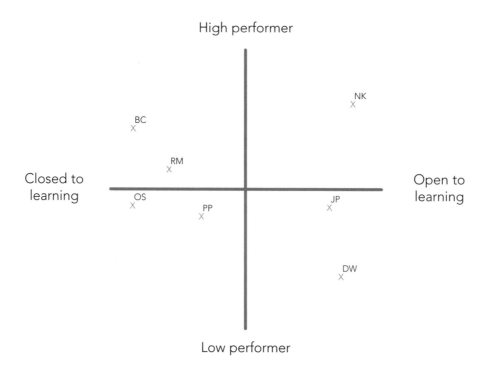

High performer

NK
X

BC
X

RM
X

Closed to
learning

Open to
learning

OS
X

PP
X

JP
X

DW
X

Low performer

Case study: Paul's team

Paul manages a team of trainers who deliver development programmes across the UK. Working with us, he used the learning–performance matrix to plot the starting points of his team. As the exercise unfolded, it quickly became apparent to him that his team members demonstrated a wide range of starting points. This was illuminating for Paul as he realised that the majority of his team were actually closed to learning. Furthermore, he recognised that some of his customers were working with trainers who were not high performers.

> However, the process of establishing the starting points had one last step to go. We asked Paul to provide evidence to justify why he had placed each of these individuals where he had. This challenge wasn't designed to undermine Paul by doubting his judgement. Instead, it was intended to ensure that the starting points were based on carefully considered evidence, not flawed perception.

In recent years, there have been some valuable contributions from cognitive psychology in the field of judgement and decision making. In particular, Nobel Prize winner Daniel Kahneman's work has shone a glaring light on just how poor humans can be when evaluating the performance of others.[6]

So, what is your judgement on where you think each individual in your team is starting from? Pay particular attention to whether your assessment may have been influenced by unconscious biases or unrepresentative and selective evidence.

Edward Thorndike coined the expression the 'halo effect' to represent the positive unconscious bias that we apply to certain people or situations.[7] Where leaders rate a person in their team highly, Thorndike's research showed that they were more likely to discount or ignore any negative feedback about that person in the future. A corollary of this is the less well-known 'horn effect', which operates in reverse.[8]

Both of these effects result from leaders developing a bias based on early or first impressions. All too frequently this preconception blinds them from seeking further information which would better inform their view of the individual's performance. The bias becomes the prism through which they interpret feedback about that person. Like it or not, we tend to hear what we are listening out for,

---

6   *The Observer*, 'Daniel Kahneman Changed the Way We Think About Thinking. But What Do Other Thinkers Think of Him?' (16 February 2014). Available at: https://www.theguardian.com/science/2014/feb/16/daniel-kahneman-thinking-fast-and-slow-tributes.

7   Edward Lee Thorndike, 'A Constant Error in Psychological Ratings', *Journal of Applied Psychology*, 4(1) (1920), 25–29.

8   Nagesh Belludi, 'The Halo and Horns Effects (Rating Errors)', *RightAttitudes.com* (30 April 2010). Available at: http://www.rightattitudes.com/2010/04/30/rating-errors-halo-effect-horns-effect.

rather than what is said. Kahneman coined the acronym WYSIATI for this bias, which stands for 'What you see is all there is'.[9] He argues that too often judgements are formed without considering whether there may be other information available that could better nuance our thinking.

These biases result in leaders overstating the extent to which a person is seen as open or closed to learning. A rushed conversation with a tired and overworked colleague who doesn't seem particularly open to learning at 5.30 p.m. on a Friday afternoon may not be representative of his or her true disposition. Similarly, a fast-paced, confidently delivered presentation doesn't prove that a particular team member is a high performer. High performers, by their nature, are authentic and consistent. This is encapsulated by Simon Sinek: 'Authenticity is more than speaking. It's also about doing. Every decision we make says something about who we are.'[10]

We have found that leaders who take the time to gain feedback from a wide range of sources, and listen to and observe their team more carefully, are less likely to fall foul of unconscious bias. We strongly recommend that leaders populate the learning–performance matrix with evidence that justifies their judgement.

So, with a clear understanding of the potential for cognitive bias, Paul decided that he needed at least three pieces of evidence to help him make an informed judgement about each individual's starting point. He added this information to his matrix. It meant that his completed matrix looked like the one following:

---

9   Daniel Kahneman, *Thinking, Fast and Slow* (London: Penguin, 2011), pp. 85–88.
10 See https://twitter.com/simonsinek/status/177849647614799873.

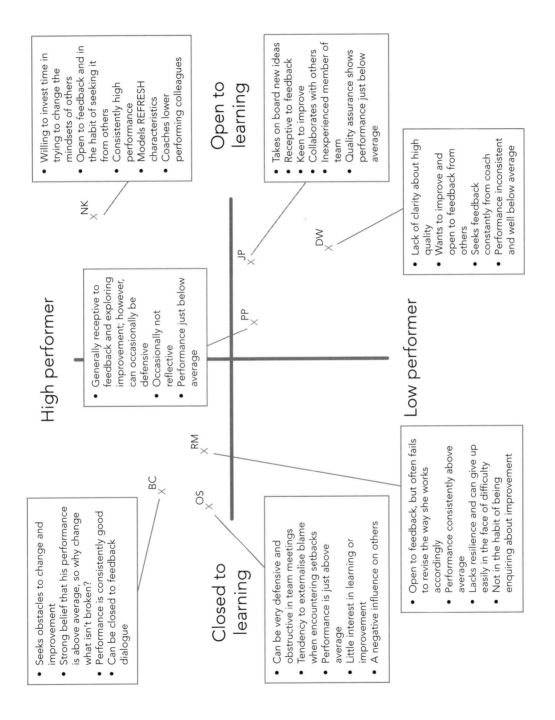

High performer

Open to
learning

Low performer

Closed to
learning

NK

- Willing to invest time in trying to change the mindsets of others
- Open to feedback and in the habit of seeking it from others
- Consistently high performance
- Models REFRESH characteristics
- Coaches lower performing colleagues

JP

- Takes on board new ideas
- Receptive to feedback
- Keen to improve
- Collaborates with others
- Inexperienced member of team
- Quality assurance shows performance just below average

DW

- Lack of clarity about high quality
- Wants to improve and open to feedback from others
- Seeks feedback constantly from coach
- Performance inconsistent and well below average

PP

- Generally receptive to feedback and exploring improvement; however, can occasionally be defensive
- Occasionally not reflective
- Performance just below average

RM

- Open to feedback, but often fails to revise the way she works accordingly
- Performance consistently above average
- Lacks resilience and can give up easily in the face of difficulty
- Not in the habit of being enquiring about improvement

BC

- Seeks obstacles to change and improvement
- Strong belief that his performance is above average, so why change what isn't broken?
- Performance is consistently good
- Can be closed to feedback dialogue

OS

- Can be very defensive and obstructive in team meetings
- Tendency to externalise blame when encountering setbacks
- Performance is just above average
- Little interest in learning or improvement
- A negative influence on others

Significantly, Paul's more careful analysis of his team led him to reassess the starting points of three of them. After consideration, OS was actually an above-average performer. Paul confided that OS's negativity in team meetings had distorted his own perception of his overall performance. This was a perfect example of the horn effect at work. Also, Paul found that PP and NK were actually more open to learning than his initial gut instinct had given them credit for; indeed, on reflection he also assessed that NK wasn't far off having the high performer KASH that he had outlined earlier on in the process.

For Paul, like other leaders who have plotted their team's starting points, the matrix provided clarity on how far away he was from having a team of high performers who were open to learning.

Reflection questions

Where would you position each of your team on the learning–performance matrix?

What evidence would you be able to provide to justify the positions you have chosen?

If you had carried out this exercise a year ago, would any of your team have been in a different position?

Are there any patterns to the distribution of where your team are positioned?

How far away are they from being a high performing and open-to-learning team?

What next?

The high performer KASH has been established and the starting points of your team have been established on the learning–performance matrix. The likelihood is that there is a gap between where the ideal team would be positioned (i.e. clustered in the top-right quadrant) and where the individuals in your team are currently. For now, just imagine what it would be like working with a team which had a profile like this one on the learning–performance matrix:

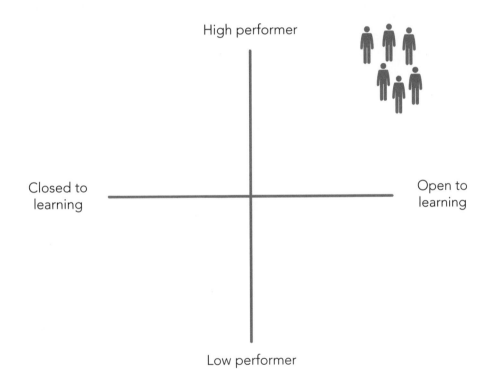

Teams don't get here without hard work and high quality training. Most teams have individuals who are either low performing or somewhat closed to learning. If this is the case, we strongly suggest that you move straight to Part II, where we analyse three of the most common barriers which cause individuals to be closed to learning and offer strategies to reduce their impact. It is essential to remove these barriers, otherwise any plan to develop effective learning in your team will be likely to fail. Just like a driver revving the engine of a car stuck in thick mud, every application of the throttle will cause the car to sink deeper.

If you are fortunate enough to have all or most of your team positioned in the open-to-learning side of the matrix, then Part II will help both you and them to consolidate and enhance their skills. Just as a runner has to maintain fitness by training regularly, so a leader has to work to maintain an open-to-learning team. People, markets and contexts change. The world we live in is volatile, uncertain, complex, ambiguous and is unlikely to slow down any time soon. In order to stay alert and agile, it pays to be connected to ongoing learning to ensure that all barriers to it are minimised or removed. We know of one leader who has the well-known Eric Hoffer quote pinned to his door for this very reason: 'In a time of drastic change, it is the learners who inherit the future. The learned usually find themselves equipped to live in a world that no longer exists.'[11]

In Part III, we will provide a clear structure to support you to design highly effective learning for your team – learning that will meet the development needs of all the individuals in your team, regardless of their starting points and regardless of the future uncertainties your organisation or team may encounter.

REFRESH reading list

Some suggested reading if you want to delve deeper:

Kegan, Robert and Lahey, Lisa Laskow (2009). *Immunity to Change: How to Overcome It and Unlock the Potential in Yourself and Your Organization* (Boston, MA: Harvard Business Review Press).

Lencioni, Patrick M. (2002). *The Five Dysfunctions of a Team: A Leadership Fable* (J-B Lencioni Series) (San Francisco, CA: Jossey-Bass).

Marcum, David and Smith, Steven (2007). *Egonomics: What Makes Ego Our Greatest Asset (Or Most Expensive Liability)* (New York: Simon & Schuster).

Pink, Daniel H. (2010). *Drive: The Surprising Truth About What Motivates Us* (Edinburgh: Canongate).

Syed, Matthew (2015). *Black Box Thinking: The Surprising Truth About Success* (London: John Murray).

---

11 Eric Hoffer, *Reflections on the Human Condition* (New York: Harper & Row, 1972), p. 22.

Part II
Overcoming barriers to learning

Two gardeners rented neighbouring allotments. One of them was impatient and lacked expertise. He strode out on the first sunny spring morning and started sowing seeds carelessly with the misplaced expectation of a bumper harvest of vegetables later in the summer.

His neighbour took a different approach. She knew that the more preparation she put in before sowing her seeds, the greater the chance that her efforts would pay dividends later on. First, she carefully weeded the beds. Then, with a pair of shears, she cut back the overgrown hedge – allowing more direct sunlight to reach the allotment and warm the soil. Finally, before sowing, she carefully raked over the soil to remove any stones.

One gardener was destined to augment his poor harvest with frozen veg from the local supermarket, while the other would be having a surplus of tasty home-grown produce.

As with gardening, so with learning. Creating the ideal conditions in which learning can flourish in a team is crucially important. This requires leaders to ensure that the ground is fertile by removing the barriers that are the equivalent of the horticulturist's weeds and pests. After all, if the conditions for learning aren't ideal, then it will be more difficult to improve the performance of your team.

- Have you ever wondered why learning is flourishing in other teams, but not yours?

- Are you puzzled why some of your team have become closed to learning?

- Are you keen to nurture fertile conditions for your team's learning?

In Part II, we will analyse the three most significant (and common) barriers that can cause individuals in a team to become closed to learning:

1   **Processing overload.** Processing overload is characterised by a feeling within the team, perhaps for different reasons, that the time or energy for learning or improvement is not available. It may be that there aren't sufficient opportunities for the team to collaborate and reflect on more effective ways to improve. Alternatively, it could be that they are operating in an environment where there is simply information overload – so much so that individuals feel completely overwhelmed and don't have the bandwidth to process anything new. When a frenetic pace of operations becomes the norm, even the most committed learner will find it hard to discover the space and time to learn. At worst, he or she may even lose the learning habit. In learning situations when

individual learners receive too much new information at once or have to perform too many tasks simultaneously, this processing overload is known as cognitive overload.

2   **Low relational trust**. Trust is crucial for learning to take place. By this we mean both the trust between team members as well as between the team and their leader. High trust within a team is like oxygen for learning. Low trust can make individuals less willing to ask questions when they are unclear. It can make them fearful about making mistakes or worry about how they will be perceived by others. Low trust can also lead to reticence about seeking and giving honest feedback. The giving and receiving of quality feedback is essential to improved performance, greater motivation and heightened trust.

3   **Perception gaps.** Perception gaps compare an individual's assessment of his or her performance to the reality of their actual performance. Different perception gaps can affect individuals in different ways. For example, they may overestimate or underestimate their performance, or the quality of the feedback they receive may be poor and demotivating. Either way, the net result may be that they become closed to learning. For instance, those with an inflated sense of their own performance can suffer from inertia. They 'know' there is no compelling need to improve because they feel more than comfortable with their performance level. On the other hand, others may perceive themselves to be at a lower level of performance than is the case. They often lack confidence and even resist feedback contrary to their perceptions because they don't think they will be up to coping with the additional challenge of new learning.

Each of the chapters in this part will offer further details about how these barriers inhibit learning, outline the reasons why they develop, and provide practical tools and strategies to overcome them.

Three-in-one and one-in-three

When processing capacity is nurtured, and when strong relational trust and accurate self-perception are all in place, the conditions for open learning are present. They are like the three legs of a stable, well-constructed stool – supporting the conditions for powerful and successful development.

There are three distinct dangers to guard against when the barriers described on pages 49–50 emerge. First, the presence of any one of these difficulties within a team has the same impact on learning as removing a leg from our stool: it loses stability and will quickly unbalance and fall over. It is very important, therefore, to ensure that none of these barriers are allowed to develop, otherwise individuals can become closed to learning.

Second, in our experience, these three barriers develop if there aren't explicit systems and norms in place to prevent them. As we have seen, these barriers are like weeds in a garden, and if left to grow unchecked will strangle the plants we want to foster and encourage. Teams that create fertile conditions for learning do not do so by accident. There has been ongoing, deliberate and conscientious work carried out by the leader, or the team itself, to ensure that these weeds can't develop.

Finally, the barriers are not usually found in isolation. For example, where processing overload is a significant impediment to learning, relational trust issues will often exist too. Team members frequently attribute the causes of processing overload to the perceived failings of their leaders. As one frustrated, overloaded and very definitely closed-to-learning individual put it: 'The problem in our place is that management haven't got a clue what they're doing. That's why we're always firefighting.' But while confronting these barriers might seem to be a major undertaking, be reassured: as the barriers tend to be interdependent, working to remove or reduce one barrier will often produce a simultaneous effect on the other two.

To aid reflection on these important issues, and to help you identify actions to start and stop doing, we have provided an action plan template at the end of each of the following three chapters.

Case study: building foundations for learning

Michelle leads an organisation of more than fifty people and has done so for the last two years. The previous incumbent had left after only six months. He had completely lost the confidence of the directors and the employees. It had become an organisation as closed to learning as we have ever encountered. Not only that, but large perception gaps had also grown. As one person put it: 'If this place were as good as some people around here think it is, we'd be world beaters.'

Michelle's first actions were to build strong relational trust, mainly through role modelling and conducting an extensive listening exercise within the organisation. She realised that the employees had been badly damaged by what had happened before she arrived. After the first six months of her tenure, she began to notice that more and more staff were becoming open to learning and, as a consequence, their openness to feedback grew too. This enabled Michelle to begin to realign perceptions with reality, and ensure that a collective realisation that things needed to change for the better could begin to emerge.

Being open to others' perceptions

Jared, a leader we greatly respect, once remarked: 'This is what I think the problems are in the team, but suppose I'm wrong ...' Given the dangers of making judgements based on selective evidence or unconscious bias (as outlined in Chapter 2), we encourage leaders to gather feedback from their teams about their views on the size and scale of the barriers to learning.

We have set up a free, anonymised survey tool (http://www.learningimperative.co.uk/learning-survey) which enables leaders to get feedback from their team about the extent to which the three barriers exist in their organisation. The summarised report provides you with detailed feedback from your team in two key areas: (1) the extent of each of the three barriers to an individual's learning, and why, and (2) what the three most important changes are that would improve learning in the team. This survey can also be found in Appendix 1.

 Reflection questions on the survey results

Once you have collated the results, here are five questions to reflect on before you move on to the next chapter:

Which barriers pose the biggest obstacles to being open to learning in your team?

What reasons could lie behind the size and scale of these barriers?

How different is your own perception of these barriers to your team's perception?

What has been your own contribution to the size of these barriers?

If you repeated this survey in a year's time, what would you like it to report?

Chapter 3

Processing overload

Dave walked into a conference at which I (Mark) was speaking. He was the team leader in a public sector organisation based in Manchester. I welcomed him and we shook hands. As he squeezed my hand he fixed me with a steely gaze for what seemed an unusually long time. 'Morning,' he said, finally. 'No offence, but I'm not really looking forward to today – I've got enough acronyms already.' During the coffee break I made a beeline for him. 'How was the morning?' I tentatively enquired. 'Oh, really good,' was his response. As he seemed happier, I enquired about the reason for our encounter at the start of the day. He slumped down in the nearest chair and unburdened the woes of his job.

His organisation was under pressure to improve. Results in his team had been stubbornly mediocre. Consequently, he and his team had been endlessly scrutinised and given mountains of 'guidance' from a host of different external consultants and quality assurance managers. Much of this advice seemed contradictory and confusing. 'We're all overwhelmed,' he said. 'How can we possibly fit in all the things we have been told to do on a daily basis? So, I've just told the team to keep doing what they know best.'

Dave showed me the list of all this well-intentioned guidance, which he kept in a little black notebook. As I read through, I reflected that there was an awful lot of it. His advice to his staff therefore had some merit. There was too much to do. It was a classic case of processing overload becoming a barrier to learning, and as a result it was a barrier to improving performance.

■ Have you ever felt people in your team can't seem to see the wood for the trees?

- Have you ever been faced with colleagues saying, 'We've got no time to embrace this change'?

- Does it ever seem that you don't have enough hours in the day to get things done?

- Have you ever wondered why some individuals in your team are able to swim in this environment, while others drown?

What's in this chapter for me?

In this chapter, we will examine processing overload and its causes. We will then identify tools and strategies to help you to create norms and habits that ensure your team have sufficient processing time, as well as plenty of energy and enthusiasm, for working on learning and improvement.

What do we mean by processing overload?

Processing overload is an umbrella term for the inability of individuals or teams to absorb new information because their processing powers have been overwhelmed. If you want to experience processing overload for yourself, just sit in on a conversation where three people are all talking simultaneously. Most of us can only effectively process information generated by a maximum of two people talking at once.[1] Perhaps you are already thinking of certain colleagues who, after one coffee too many, could provide you with processing overload all on their own!

Processing overload can also be caused by trying to perform two or more challenging tasks at the same time – for example, when driving in difficult conditions or unfamiliar places, we might well ask our passengers to stop talking or turn down the radio so we can concentrate better. In normal conditions, of course, driving is largely performed on autopilot as we focus our attention on processing the conversation or on the content of the radio programme.

---

1   See Mihaly Csikszentmihalyi and Isabella Selega Csikszentmihalyi, *Optimal Experience: Psychological Studies of Flow in Consciousness* (New York: Cambridge University Press, 1992), pp. 17–18.

Why does processing overload act as a barrier to learning?

For those of us seeking to grow and develop, the hard reality is that learning is effortful. Indeed, the more complex the learning, the more effort is required. John Sweller calls this effortful processing 'cognitive load'.[2] When the cognitive load becomes too great, barriers to learning arise – which can be either conscious or unconscious.

At the conscious level, the reaction can be similar to that of Dave and his team described at the start of this chapter. They feel unable to process any new information because they are already 'maxed out'. Whether their perception is accurate or not, it acts as their reality. This can create a mindset whereby learning and improvement are not possible because individuals have erected obstacles to learning and are actively resisting new information. Sometimes, it is only those who are prepared to carve out time from their private lives who might have a chance to absorb the information. This feeling of overwhelmedness is not just a barrier to learning. It can also have a damaging emotional and physical impact on individuals too. On many occasions, we have observed raised levels of stress and anxiety, often leading to higher levels of absenteeism, as a result of processing overload.

As we made clear in the previous chapter, this sense of being overwhelmed can seriously affect relational trust and perception gaps. This is why we are so convinced that the avoidance of processing overload is an essential aspect of effective learning. We would go so far as to say that every successful organisation we have had the privilege to work in has determinedly focused on tackling the problem of processing overload in order to improve performance.

Processing overload can also hamper learning on an unconscious level. This is the problem caused by the incorrect filtering of new information – again because we haven't got the bandwidth to process all the new learning. This leads to the danger of our selective filtering causing us to make incorrect interpretations. When we suffer this kind of processing overload, we are also prone to make the assumption that others are interpreting new information in the same way we are.

---

2   John Sweller, 'Cognitive Load Theory, Learning Difficulty, and Instructional Design', *Learning and Instruction*, 4(4) (1994), 295–312.

When information is new to us, it is very easy to make false but perfectly logical connections, as we will explain.

The questions 'Do you understand?' and 'Does this make sense?' may well fail to expose what has, or has not, been understood. Understanding may have taken place, but it could be quite different from what was intended. An amusing anecdote illustrates this point well. Some years ago a teacher on one of our teacher development programmes recounted how one of his students had listened intently to his explanation of how the Romans moved around Europe extending their empire. In his history project, the student wrote that 'they were called Romans because they never stayed in one place for very long'! The child, overwhelmed with information about the topic, had made his own incorrect yet perfectly rational interpretation.

What are the main causes of processing overload?

In this section, working from our analysis both of high performing teams and those who are struggling to improve, we will examine the most significant causes of processing overload. This should help you do two things: (1) diagnose possible reasons for processing overload in your own team, and (2) enable you to prevent processing overload from developing in the future.

Lack of shared clarity

In the absence of shared clarity, the risk of excessive performance variability grows within a team. This variability can lead to time and resources being diverted to fixing or remedying the resulting problems. Time and again, leaders we have interviewed or worked with who have successfully developed the performance of their teams, have insisted that shared clarity lies at the core of their drive for improvement. One such leader, Joanne, reflected on the transformational impact that investing time in the building of shared clarity had made on her own team.

When she first took over her role she realised that her team were suffering from huge processing overload. This was mostly caused by the team having to firefight issues on a daily basis, mostly due to the poor quality of their work. The team were stressed and morale was low. Her first action was to step back and analyse the underlying causes of the problem. All the symptoms consistently linked back to a lack of shared clarity. She realised that creating this clarity had to be the team's first task on the journey towards excellence.

Breaking out of the downward spiral of processing overload can be a knotty and difficult challenge for teams whose leaders are too busy to take the time to reflect and analyse. The steps needed to introduce clarity have to be carefully thought through and sensitively applied if they are to be successful.

No sane leader sets out to create a lack of clarity about vision, goals and objectives within their team. However, the fact is that leaders of many organisations and teams are not at all clear about what is required. They are leaders who don't invest sufficient time to set clear expectations. As one vice-president of a global beauty brand told us, 'Our leaders focus on tasks and results, not on creating shared clarity. As a result, our people are constantly burning out, as what they are asked to do each time changes.'

In addition, many leaders tend to make incorrect assumptions about the degree of shared clarity. These assumptions are often based on little or no evidence and lead to a kind of blindness about what is really going on. Two main factors lead to over-optimistic assumptions:

1   **Underestimating complexity.** In some teams, the illusion of shared clarity exists due to the presence of superficial rubrics and policy documents. The vagueness of such documents can lead to different interpretations of what the words mean and how the processes should be carried out, particularly across different contexts. Too often, the values that underpin the policies are not clearly understood either. What this means in practice is that the quality level of the work mainly depends on who in the team is doing the task and whether or not they have understood what is required.

2   **Ineffective communication.** The quality of dialogue among team members is just as important as frequency, perhaps even more so. A team can meet every day, but if the quality of dialogue is poor then the likelihood of misunderstanding and confusion remains. We have heard leaders blame lack of shared clarity on the fact that team members travel extensively and don't often meet up. Yet we've encountered many teams who work remotely and actually have greater shared clarity than teams who work together in the same building. When leaders and managers assume too much, they may well

have made the mistake of believing that teaching and telling are the same as learning and understanding. As we noted earlier in the chapter, the meaning we take as a listener can be quite different from that intended by the speaker.

 ## Case study: embedding a lack of shared clarity

Sitting in a large meeting, the team leader outlined all the key priorities for the month ahead and the non-negotiables everyone had to follow. A quality assurance visit was looming and everyone was under pressure to ensure that it went well. The meeting overran, so there was no time for questions or discussion about the large number of items that required improvement.

Later, over coffee, some of those who had been present were reflecting on what had been said. What surprised them was how they had each taken away quite different interpretations of what needed to be done. Similarly, there was little consensus about how they should apply the non-negotiables in their work. With the important quality assurance visit looming, this meeting had proved a very ineffective platform for delivering shared understanding, consistency or clarity of purpose.

Have you ever been in a similar meeting where vast amounts of new information was shared without there being any opportunity to dialogue, question, challenge or create shared meaning?

Ineffective prioritisation

We have heard the plaintive cry many times from individuals in teams: 'We simply haven't got time for new learning!' What seems on the surface to be a shortage of time is often a case of ineffective prioritisation. In some teams, this situation can be a short-term or seasonal feature, while in others it is seemingly a day-to-day norm.

Two problems that can exacerbate processing overload are a long to-do list and focusing on starting new tasks rather than completing old ones. Where a team or individual is not able to prioritise effectively, and trying to work on too many tasks at once, processing overload is an inevitable result.

Novice/expert distinction

'What is everybody complaining about?' was the baffled response of one team leader. Stuart simply didn't recognise processing overload as an issue in his team, despite feedback indicating that it was from a survey he had conducted with them. Processing overload was the elephant in the room. It was the big barrier to his team's learning and development.

Stuart's response was understandable because he himself wasn't suffering from processing overload.[3] He had underestimated how much his own expertise had enabled him to manage the processing load that came with the job. Stuart was a high performer. It was one of the reasons he had been appointed as team leader. Conversely, his team were largely inexperienced and consequently were low performers. They were less able to process and make sense of the high volume of information that Stuart could handle.

The greater the lack of experience and expertise, the higher the likelihood of processing overload occurring – unless it is well managed. Consequently, it is those in the shaded zone of the learning–performance matrix (see page 62) who will be most adversely affected by processing overload. And, of course, these are the individuals whose performance most needs to be improved.

---

3   An example of the differences between how novices and experts process information was demonstrated in chess by Herbert A. Simon and Kevin J. Gilmartin, 'A Simulation Memory for Chess Positions', *Cognitive Psychology*, 5(1) (1973), 29–46.

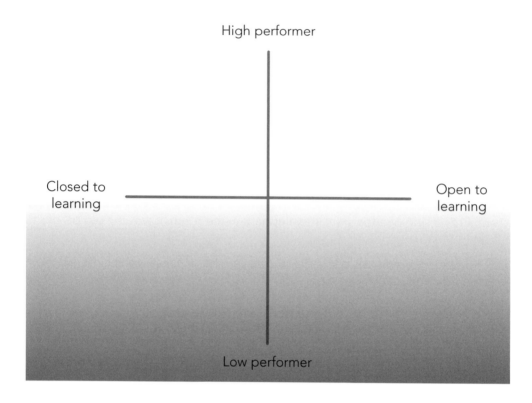

High performer

Closed to learning   Open to learning

Low performer

An environment of distractions

For many individuals and teams, a significant and growing cause of processing overload is the nature of work, and in particular the environment in which work is carried out. Most modern workplaces are awash with distractions and often don't give individuals much opportunity for reflection, enquiry or quiet, focused attention to a specific task. Some of these distractions may be human interactions. However, we have found that the predominant distraction is access to a wide range of communication technologies, such as mobile phones, email, the internet and other networking software. This often leads to individuals undertaking multiple tasks at the same time, under the illusion that more work can be done in the same amount of time.

Recent research has shown that multitasking is actually an extremely inefficient way of working and can actually slow down productivity. It is part of what entrepreneur Joe Kraus bemoans when he argues that 'We're creating a culture of distraction'.[4] Switching between tasks, such as checking emails while trying to read or compose a report, causes a strain on the brain as it has to constantly reset its focus. Furthermore, multitasking requires the brain to make more decisions and to question priorities. Queries arise such as: does this email require an instant response? Who else needs to know about this? Given its brevity, does this email have an underlying, unspoken message? These competing questions add to the potential for distraction and stress. And it isn't only the process of multitasking that creates cognitive strain; the very opportunity to multitask has the potential to lower performance.

The unfortunate consequence of a distraction-rich environment and the ineffective use of multitasking is that by lunchtime some individuals may feel a greater sense of processing overload than they did when they started that morning.

It's not just about work, work, work

We need to bear in mind that our colleagues have important roles to play in the world outside work. They might be sons, daughters, partners, parents, friends or relatives. This web of human connection plays a key role in maintaining and recharging the energy of everyone in the team. But these roles can also create cognitive strain when challenges and crises occur. Bereavement, sickness and the breakdown of relationships inevitably cause stress and impinge on the quality of an individual's work.

---

4   See Justin Rubio, 'Google Ventures' Joe Kraus: "We're Creating a Culture of Distraction" ', *The Verge* (29 May 2012). Available at: https://www.theverge.com/2012/5/29/3050625/google-ventures-joe-kraus-culture-distractions-presentation.

Reflection questions on survey results

On page 53 we offered you a tool to gain feedback on the three barriers to learning. Now is a good time, if you carried out the survey, to reflect on the answers to questions 1–8.

To what extent is processing overload a barrier to learning in your team?

Which particular issues were flagged up by your team?

Did any aspects of the feedback surprise you?

For questions to which feedback was positive, what has been your own contribution to achieving this?

What are the key actions required as a result of this feedback?

Strategies to reduce processing overload

Given the causes outlined above, we have identified three interdependent strategies to reduce the impact of processing overload in teams. First, models of excellence are necessary so that teams can gain shared clarity – they need to see what they are being expected to create and how best to achieve it. Second, tasks and projects must be prioritised effectively so that there is sufficient capacity available to streamline the workflow. Lastly, reflective dialogue, questioning and active listening are required to ensure that everyone has the knowledge, understanding and processing capacity for learning and for taking effective action. We will explore each of these three strategies in more detail on the pages that follow.

Modelling excellence

Why do some teams and organisations suffer from a lack of shared clarity about excellence? This is a question we have pondered at length over years of working to improve capacity and performance within teams. Whenever we have encountered a lack of shared clarity, there are two issues that occur again and again.

The first is that leaders have not defined clearly what they mean by excellence. What does it look and sound like? What are the processes and principles that need to be followed in order to achieve it? The consequence of this lack of clarity from leaders is confusion, often resulting in team members looking busy but working ineffectively.

The second issue is that there may be clarity among the leadership, but it is not communicated effectively to the team. Indeed, this isn't a single conversation. The entire team, whether they are high performers or low performers, novices or experts, need to be engaged in an ongoing dialogue about what best practice represents.

We have gathered together some tools and strategies that have been proven to develop shared clarity, and which address both of these issues.

Making models for excellence visible

The old adage that 'a picture tells a thousand words' has a strong grounding in cognitive science.[5] We receive information primarily through two sensory pathways – auditory and visual. It makes sense to support verbal input with images that exemplify the key concepts and ideas that need to be grasped and embodied. Visual representations of excellence can include illustrations, decision trees, diagrams and flow charts (see example on page 66), as well as photographs, animations or video clips showcasing high performance in action. The basic principle is to ensure that the behaviours and attitudes which support excellence are fully deconstructed. In doing so, novices and lower performers can gain clarity about the thinking patterns and processes they need to replicate in order to match the performance levels of their higher performing peers.

---

5   See, for example: https://www.psychologistworld.com/memory/cognitive-load-theory.

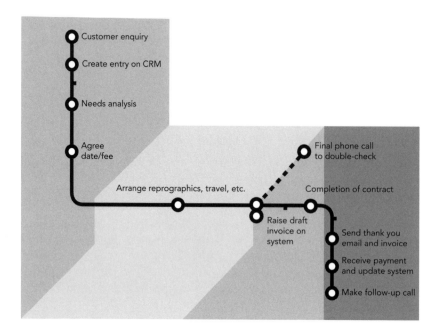

Case study: modelling excellence

A group of novice coaches at a top sports club were eager to improve the effectiveness of the video analysis sessions they led with their teams. The head of coaching was keen that this potentially powerful tool for reflection and improvement was fully utilised, so he filmed one of his high performing coaches leading an exemplar video analysis session and then replayed it to the novices. They were blown away by the quality of what they saw. Not only was the focus of the discussion between coach and team much sharper than their own, but the quality of reflection by the players was also much deeper and ultimately more impactful on performance. They finished the training session much clearer about what excellence looked and sounded like, and how to achieve it.

Of course, when considering models of excellence the most important model is yourself. As Albert Schweitzer once said, 'Example is not the main thing. It is the only thing.'[6] Modelling excellence exemplifies the authenticity of our behaviours and attitudes and powerfully projects the idea that these standards apply to all, regardless of their position in the team, as the following anecdote illustrates.

A regional manager of a large retail chain recounted her sense of shame during a quality assurance check at one of the company's stores. In this firm there is a zero tolerance rule for staff phones on the shop floor. Embarrassingly, a phone started ringing as she was standing next to the tills. It was hers – she had forgotten to turn it off on arrival! She told us she just wanted the ground to open up and swallow her as the store manager and supervisor cast her disapproving looks. She quickly apologised to all for the poor example she had set.

Spot the difference

Creating regular opportunities for teams to compare and contrast examples of excellence with suboptimal performance can play a key role in ensuring shared clarity of process and outcome. This can really help to demystify what excellence means and facilitate rich dialogue and analysis about the causes of optimal and suboptimal performance, and what needs to be done to ensure that lessons are carried into the future.

Case study: 'eureka' moment about clarity

A leader was moaning to us about variability in the quality of report writing among his team: 'Some think they're writing *War and Peace*, while others leave me needing psychoactive drugs to help me piece together their meaning.' When we asked if he had ever showed them examples of what he meant by an 'excellent' report, it was clear that this simple strategy had not

---

6   Eugene Exman, 'God's Own Man' [interview with Albert Schweitzer], *United Nations World Magazine*, 6(1) (1952), p. 34.

been on his solution radar. He went straight to the copier and compiled examples of good, bad and downright ugly reports for his team to rank and compare. 'Thanks,' he said excitedly. 'Now I've got a great focus for this afternoon's team meeting.'

Think-alouds

Not everything that constitutes excellence is visible. One leader we worked with suggested that only 10% of what underpinned excellence in his team was visible or audible. Much of the excellence stemmed from the internal thinking processes and non-verbal cues used by the high performers. Think-alouds are a training strategy that make the internal processes of excellence transparent to others. They invite high performers to share out loud their thinking processes, decision making strategies and reasons for their actions and behaviours as they carry out a task.

For example, we might be impressed by a trainer's thought-provoking questions in a session which took the delegates' learning to a much deeper level. However, these questions are just the tip of the iceberg. What needs to be surfaced is the internal process that led the trainer to formulate these particular excellent questions. Inviting the trainer, or any other modeller, to think aloud during a video replay of the session, and explain his or her inner process, helps others to understand how they can develop their own awareness and skills. Think-alouds can also help to decode the following elements:

- What awareness caused the high performer to choose one particular strategy over another?

- How did the high performer create such a high level of trust with the client/customer/group of participants so they were able to speak so openly and frankly?

- What impact did the physical nature of the environment that the high performer organised have on the success of the outcome?

Think-alouds support novices and low performers to understand the changes they need to make in their KASH. The transparency of the process enables them to overcome the frustration of seeing excellence in action, but not knowing how the rabbit is removed from the hat. They help to demystify the magic of excellence. Technically, think-alouds make explicit our metacognition – how we think about our thinking.[7] They provide an ideal scaffold for less expert team members to develop their performance. They also invite us to enquire further when we see excellence happening in front of us and need to know, 'How exactly do you do that?'

Effective prioritisation

'If only we had more time we could crack the processing overload problem you've uncovered,' was Sally's slightly unconvincing reflection. Her team were struggling. They were all working long hours but didn't seem to be improving their output. In a similar organisation, just two miles down the road, another team with a comparable workload were thriving. It wasn't lack of time that was holding Sally's team back, it was poor prioritisation. Effective prioritisation, which the competitor was using, would have provided Sally's team with the time to develop shared clarity and consequently more effective and sustainable performance.

Kanban

There are many tools available to develop skills in prioritisation and workload management. However, there is one we favour which seems to tick all the crucial boxes in terms of reducing processing overload. It also has the advantage that it can be used by both individuals and whole teams. The strategy is called kanban, which translates literally from the Japanese as 'signboard'. It was developed by Japanese firms to manage workflow. Kanban is a deceptively simple tool which has four important principles that give it a massive advantage over traditional to-do lists:

1   Writing down every task that needs to be completed removes the need to remember everything in your head, freeing up cognitive space.

2   Only after all the work to do has been identified can effective prioritisation take place.

---

7   See Janet Metcalfe and Arthur P. Shimamura, *Metacognition: Knowing About Knowing* (Cambridge, MA: MIT Press, 1994).

3   Processing overload is avoided by identifying which tasks require immediate focus and attention, which tasks are in the pipeline and which tasks can be put on hold.

4   The obsessive focus of the team is always on the completion of existing tasks, rather than the unfocused starting of new ones.

Building your own kanban system involves just four easy steps:

Step 1: Write down, on separate sticky notes, *all* the individual tasks that need to be completed. It is important to add an estimated timescale for how long each task will take to complete and a deadline for completion. Here's an example:

It is crucial that every single task is logged, with absolutely no exceptions. There are two reasons for this: first, writing down every task means the brain no longer needs to remember them, thus freeing up memory space and providing clarity, and, second, effective prioritisation requires that all information is available at the point of sorting.

Handy hint: It is much more effective to chunk down large tasks into smaller, more manageable tasks on separate sticky notes. This is because it is easier to estimate the time it takes to complete smaller tasks.

Step 2: Using the four columns below, neatly arrange all the sticky notes in the waiting column. At this stage it may seem as though all that has been created is a very colourful to-do list; however, there is a significant difference. The waiting column is the place where you go to select every single new task that you plan to work on each day. It is also where you will add any new tasks that arise in the future.

Waiting	Action	Holding	Done

The advantage of the kanban process is that, if you follow it correctly, it is impossible to be overwhelmed by work. Each day, you will make choices about which tasks you are going to transfer from the waiting column into the action column, which is for tasks that are going to be worked on to completion that day. This choice will be informed both by those tasks which have top priority (i.e. a combination of importance and deadline) and, most importantly, those that can be completed during the time available in the day. If there are only four hours available due to meetings or other commitments, then only four hours' worth of tasks can be transferred into the action column. This avoids the curse of multitasking outlined earlier in the chapter, where individuals find themselves mentally jumping from one uncompleted task to another without finishing any of them.

The kanban process demands self-discipline to prioritise the focus for that day based on the tasks in the action column, without being distracted by other tasks in the waiting column or any new tasks that suddenly materialise. This discipline prevents the danger of multitasking from slowing task completion.

Running kanban as a team naturally creates an environment for valuable discussion, particularly around prioritisation and the allocation of time. Agreement has to be reached each day between team members and the team leader on what to move across to the action column and what to leave in the waiting column. These discussions include:

- **The allocation of tasks**: are any members of the team more overloaded than others? What might be the consequences and causes of any imbalance? Do some team members need to switch tasks to correct imbalances?

- **Prioritisation of tasks**: what are the team's priorities in terms of focus for transferring new tasks into the action column? What will be the consequences of the prioritisation decisions that have been made?

- **Work in progress**: which tasks are taking more or less time than predicted? What reasons lie behind any variance? What can we learn from this? What are the knock-on effects of any delays?

Step 3: The holding column is for any tasks that are held up because the team is waiting on information, feedback or resources from elsewhere. This both avoids frustration and prevents the action column from getting overly clogged up. It also avoids the ever-present risk of forgetting the task. An example is shown on page 73. This task is in the holding column as Mark has not yet received the phone call from CC to confirm the date/time of the meeting.

Step 4: The done column. There is something indefinably satisfying about clearing the decks of work. This rarely happens with a traditional to-do list. However, with kanban, the satisfaction of definitively completing tasks becomes the daily norm, as each day the sharp focus of the individual or team is on clearing the action column. Suddenly, work becomes doable. After all, you have selected the work to move from waiting to action based on the time available on any given day. Therefore, the processing load is much more manageable as the workload has been matched to the capacity of the team or individual. In addition, the at-a-glance visibility of the sticky notes shows that work is flowing, and the tactile experience of moving them from waiting to action or holding to done gives a satisfying sense of progress.

As work is completed, the kanban process offers more opportunities for reflection and discussion. For example:

■ What were the reasons for tasks that were completed behind schedule?

■ What were the reasons for tasks that were completed ahead of schedule?

■ What did we learn from working on these tasks?

■ Could we approach that task differently and more effectively next time?

■ Do any tasks in the waiting column need to be reprioritised as a result?

For those whose work means they are rarely in one place, and therefore can't use a physical kanban board, there are a plethora of online apps, such as Trello, which serve the same function. Many of these apps enable teams to share their planning too.

Shared clarity through dialogue

Frank and open dialogue has a hugely important role to play in creating greater clarity. As one leader we admire said, 'The key to my job is making sure that every interaction I have with my team, whether it is a one-to-one or with a larger group, prompts everyone to think more deeply about what we do, why we do it and how we can do it better.' Such ongoing dialogue can encourage:

■ Greater enquiry and effective action among the team.

■ A deepening awareness and understanding of what excellence means, and what it looks and sounds like.

■ Opportunities for the deconstruction of excellence so that the bar for excellence is raised and lower performers learn ways to narrow the gap between their own performance and that of higher performers.

In our view, any interaction between the team leader and the team is a meeting, whether it is the whole team or a one-to-one. Time and again we have found that those leaders who are most effective in reducing processing overload see *every* interaction as a valuable opportunity to develop shared clarity within their teams. As a consequence, they place great value on these meetings and plan them thoughtfully.

This makes economic sense too. Meetings cost money. One team leader we know worked out that the cost of an average meeting with his team is £1,200! He has a sticky note on his wall to remind him. He knows that he needs to plan his meetings well to get a return on his investment.

In this final section, we will explore proven strategies which team leaders use to increase the quality of interactions within their teams, particularly in pursuit of shared clarity and the reduction of processing overload.

Pre-reading

Most meetings in organisations are ineffective. The sheer amount of new information presented creates massive processing overload. The more information that is introduced, the less time there is for meaningful discussion and enquiry to create shared understanding. A useful strategy to reduce this overload is to distribute information to team members in advance, so they can pre-read and formulate their own questions and thoughts before they arrive. You don't necessarily need to send all the information; often, the big picture – the key points briefly outlined and explained – will be enough to allow participants to get their heads around it and formulate some questions.

We recently worked with a team who tested pre-reading before meetings for a month. They found a massive benefit in this simple approach. Instead of getting headaches during meetings as they tried to process huge amounts of information, they had time to discuss and come to reasoned judgements about next steps.[8] Having been totally won over to this new way of working, they agreed that in future any reports or presentation papers would be circulated at least forty-eight hours prior to meetings to give everyone the chance to read and reflect in advance.

Planning meetings backwards

'Planning backwards from the beautiful outcome' has long been our mantra with leaders and their teams. Starting at the end, by envisioning the ideal outcome, and planning backwards from it is a really effective way to ensure meetings create greater shared clarity.

Start by asking yourself some focused questions: what would be the best outcome for this meeting given the time available? What would really put a smile on everyone's face in terms of increasing shared clarity and reduced processing overload? What specific aspects of KASH are you hoping to explore in this meeting in order to create greater shared clarity?

As you plan the meeting, deliberately build in opportunities for rich dialogue. This will support shared clarity and enable you to get feedback on whether everyone has developed the level of understanding that you are seeking. Ask yourself: what thinking and discussion do I want to encourage in this meeting? Depending on the answers in the first step, some of the following discussion frameworks and questions might be appropriate for various scenarios:

- Analysing a recent event that has taken place. For example, consider a quality issue that has led to a customer complaint and use this to provide the opportunity for rich reflection on the causes of the problem. Evaluate different options to avoid a similar event happening again.

---

8 Creating the space for rich, productive dialogue to happen doesn't guarantee it will take place. There also needs to be strong relational trust in the room. This is covered in more detail in Chapter 4.

- Deconstructing models of excellence. Why is this an excellent example of how we do things in our team? What were the behaviours, strategies or thinking steps that led to the excellent outcome?

- Applying new ideas to real-life situations. How might this new strategy be implemented on a day-to-day basis in our team?

- Comparing and contrasting. What are the similarities and differences between the two options/events we are discussing?

- Ranking options. What are the pros and cons of the options we have in front of us? What other factors could help us to rank these options with greater clarity?

- Looking for patterns in information. What are the trends or patterns in the information we have in front of us? What might be the underlying causes?

- Analysing errors. What went wrong? What caused it to go wrong? How can we avoid a repeat incident?

- Linking new ideas with existing practice. How does this change how we operate? What are the connections or similarities with what we do already?

- Making predictions/forecasts. What are the likely outcomes if we take that action? What are the implications of these outcomes for our team?

- Gathering feedback from the team about their experiences of a new process that has recently been implemented.

Reflection question

In meetings you have attended recently, which of these discussion frameworks might have helped you to get better feedback about the extent of shared clarity in the room?

Fail to plan and plan to fail

A team leader we recently spoke to ruefully reflected on a meeting she had led in which these backward planning steps had not been followed. She described it as a double disaster. When asked what she meant she said, 'The first disaster was that those attending left with a complete lack of clarity about the initiative that I'd set out in the meeting. The second disaster was that I had no idea they were unclear about it.'

Reflection question

To what extent do meetings in your team raise, or reduce, processing overload and shared clarity within your team?

Building greater reflection

The major advantage of deliberately ring-fencing time for reflective and challenging dialogue is that it provides structured opportunities for lower performers to learn from the thinking and effective behaviours of higher performers. It is likely that high performers already value and practise reflective enquiry and ways to put their ideas into action. Such strategies play a key role in the ongoing development of high performers. Setting aside time for reflection also slows down the team and forces them to stop just 'doing' and instead start 'thinking about the doing'. In the most effective teams we have analysed, developing and deepening shared clarity is not an end point in itself, but an ongoing habit.

Mel, the leader of a small team in a public sector organisation, has her own spin on nurturing enquiry and action within her team. She calls it 'coffee and pastry time'. It started with her attempt to slow down her team and create a new habit. She got some resistance at the outset – comments such as 'We haven't got time for this' and 'We don't need more pointless team building' were to be heard. However, over time, the weekly Friday afternoon trip across the road to the coffee shop became something the team looked forward to. It gave them a chance to step off the treadmill and reflect on their own development and that of the team. Mel initially scaffolded the sessions using questions like these:

- What have I learned about myself this week?

- What have I learned from others?

- What has made you curious this week?

- What are the distractions present that affect your work?

- What questions have come into your head?

- What have we as a team done well? Why? How?

- What hasn't been done well?

- What can we do to improve? What can we do differently?

Over time, the scaffolds weren't needed as the dialogue in these sessions began to occur naturally. Mel was delighted when this slow thinking began to spill over into the office and permeate the day-to-day workings of the team. In particular, the two newer, lower performing members of the team commented that these sessions really helped them to better understand their roles and the challenges that were associated with them.

Conducting a pre-mortem

Just as post-mortems can help to determine the reasons behind a death, pre-mortems aim to prevent a death in the first place. In this case, we are trying to avoid a 'death' created by the implementation of a poor decision. Pre-mortems are a great discussion framework for improving the team's understanding of the potential pitfalls of any new initiative, and they also deepen the shared clarity of the team around the areas of greatest risk. Posing questions such as, 'Strategy X failed – what could have caused that to happen?' requires the team to spend time speculating about all the things that may possibly go wrong. Once this list of possible dangers has been collated, the team then move on to drawing up a series of actions/strategies which will prevent the failure from happening.

We have facilitated pre-mortems on a diverse range of topics such as 'All our new graduate recruits leave within a year', 'This new leadership course will fail to sell', 'Our new initiative to improve teaching/sales/marketing doesn't get traction' and

'Customers don't return to our stores'. Underpinning the process is a deliberate focus on getting the team to think more deeply about the wider context in which they operate, about how they act and behave, what might be the consequences of certain actions and, above all, how they can generate more analytical dialogue which supports greater shared clarity. Furthermore, pre-mortems help the experts and high performers within the team to share their deeper understanding with their novice or less expert peers.

Case study: the hot debrief

John has worked in the fire service for over thirty years. He has led hundreds of fire-fighters, and trained even more, in the UK and overseas. He is a big fan of the 'hot debrief', or post-mortem, as a tool to create greater enquiry and more effective future action within his team and to increase the depth of shared clarity. John's hot debrief is a meeting for the fire crew at the scene of the incident they have just attended. A hot debrief is most effective as close to the time of the incident as possible. They can take anything from ten minutes to an hour. The debrief forces John's crews to develop the habit of reflecting every time they attend an incident. John's crew leader colleagues tended to undertake hot debriefs a lot less than he did. Of the men and women who served with John, a far greater number progressed into leadership positions within the fire service compared to those from other crews. His insistence on hot debriefs created long lasting and effective habits of reflection within his teams.

John, and other leaders we have worked with and interviewed, realises the importance of making reflective dialogue habitual. These routines are especially useful for those who are not in the habit of 'thinking about what we do'. Over time, routines and tools such as the hot debrief and pre-mortems can improve the decision making of everyone in the team. Novices and low performers are able to quickly learn how more expert colleagues deal with situations through listening to them talk about their assessments, actions and the thinking processes behind them, backed up by experiential evidence.

Reflection questions

Are your team in the habit of reflecting regularly?

What are the costs or benefits of the answer to the question above?

In what ways do you, as a leader, model the habit of being reflective and acting on ideas generated by your enquiry?

Maintaining processing capacity action plan

What could be the key start/stop actions that will help to maintain processing capacity in your team?

What could be the start/stop actions in terms of modelling excellence for your team?

What could be the start/stop actions to ensure effective prioritisation in your team?

What could be the start/stop actions in terms of creating shared clarity through dialogue in your team?

What are the key actions you can put into practice to ensure that processing overload and lack of clarity do not act as a barrier to learning in your team?

Start actions

Stop actions

REFRESH reading list

Some suggested reading if you want to delve deeper:

Berney, Catherine (2014). *The Enlightened Organization: Executive Tools and Techniques from the World of Organizational Psychology* (London: Kogan Page).

Covey, Stephen R. (1989). *The 7 Habits of Highly Effective People* (London: Simon & Schuster).

Duhigg, Charles (2012). *The Power of Habit: Why We Do What We Do, and How to Change* (London: Random House).

Klingberg, Torkel (2009). *The Overflowing Brain: Information Overload and the Limits of Working Memory*, tr. Neil Betteridge (New York: Oxford University Press).

Newport, Cal (2016). *Deep Work: Rules for Focused Success in a Distracted World* (London: Piatkus).

Palmer, Alan (2014). *Talk Lean: Shorter Meetings. Quicker Results. Better Relations.* (Chichester: John Wiley).

Chapter 4

Low relational trust

In 2001, sitting in front of one of Mark Rothko's final paintings at the Tate Modern in London, Paul O'Hare, a painter and decorator from Liverpool, cried uncontrollably. Only a few weeks before, he had entered a TV reality show called *Faking It*. The series went on to win two BAFTAs and an International Emmy. The challenge at the centre of the programme was that people from one particular walk of life had to pass themselves off as experts in another. Examples included a Somerset vicar who had to persuade others of his credentials as an Essex-based second-hand car dealer, a punk rocker who posed as the conductor of an illustrious classical orchestra, and a sheep shearer who swapped his shears for scissors in a hairdressing salon. Paul O'Hare had to quickly learn to be a conceptual artist. Each participant was given thirty days to learn from a personal mentor as much as they could about the profession to which they aspired. The mentors' job was to build the fakers' KASH so they could become an 'expert' in a ridiculously short period of time.

One of Paul's mentors was an artist called Laura. Two days into the process, she took him to the Tate to show him works by different artists, one of which was *Black on Gray* by Mark Rothko – a canvas that (to the untrained eye) looks like a black horizontal stripe above a grey stripe. Paul thought little of the painting at the time. Twelve days later he saw it in a very different light, telling Laura, 'I see it, I see the emotion.'

Paul had learned to develop his artistic skills by working with his *Faking It* mentors and he exhibited his work alongside four artists who had each been painting and selling their art for a number of years. Paul was so successful that he completely fooled the panel of art experts who were judging the contestants. A key ingredient in Paul's success was the relationship he had with his mentors. By degrees they built greater and greater trust in each other, creating a virtuous circle of development. The relationships helped Paul to develop his skills fast enough to convince the judges, and it also had a longer-term impact.

Shortly after the programme he left his job as a painter and decorator. He successfully studied for a degree, his first ever qualification, and then set up an interior design studio. To this day he has been successfully making a full-time living from interior design and selling his art – some of it for thousands of pounds. The relationship between Paul and Laura, mentor and mentee, which was based on trust, unlocked something in Paul that he hadn't realised was there – the capacity to learn more than he had ever thought possible.

What's in this chapter for me?

First, we will examine how low relational trust negatively impacts your team's openness to learning. Then we will reflect on the strength of relational trust within your team. Finally, we will examine the key ingredients that build strong relational trust and explore proven, practical strategies to maintain the high trust required to ensure that your team remains open to learning.

What do we mean by relational trust?

In the context of this book, relational trust is the mutual connection between two or more people which enables them to feel they can be fully open to each other's questions, challenges and feedback. It is different from trust because it has an important reciprocal dimension to it. We have chosen to use the term 'relational trust' throughout this book because, if you are trying to build a team who are open to learning, then relational trust will need to exist between all its members. It is like a road traffic roundabout – for it to flow properly, all the drivers have to trust each other. In contrast, trust is more of a one-way street. We might trust our GP when we are in their surgery, but they don't have to trust us back.

The relational trust that developed between Paul and his mentor, Laura, played a crucial role in his development from low performer to high performer. Paul was able to take more risks and pose more questions without fearing how Laura would perceive him. Similarly, he was more open to listening and acting on her feedback because he believed that it was accurate and would help him to improve. For Laura's part, she was willing to invest the time in coaching and mentoring Paul because she had faith that he would listen to the advice and commit to the journey without giving up. Without this relational trust, in all likelihood Paul would still be painting and decorating.

The story of Paul's inspirational development with Laura's support exemplifies why we refer to relational trust as the 'glue' in a truly open-to-learning team. The glue doesn't just bond the leader with their team; it also bonds team members together. With strong relational trust, connections develop that hold the open-to-learning team together, even when faced with change, challenge or setbacks. We have worked with teams who have overcome huge adversity on their journey to excellence because of the strong relational trust they have forged.

- Have you ever found low relational trust to be a barrier to learning within your team?

- Are you keen to understand the causes and consequences of low relational trust?

- Would you like to know the ingredients that will strengthen the relational 'glue' in your team?

If your answer is yes to any of these questions, there are some ideas in this chapter that are guaranteed to have a positive impact on relationships within your team.

Why does low relational trust act as a barrier to learning?

Thinking back over your working life, we would like you to identify two contrasting relationships with colleagues – one relationship where you enjoyed high relational trust and another where trust was low. Reflect on each of these six questions for each relationship in turn:

1   Who was that person?

2   How was the working relationship?

3   How open and honest was your communication?

4   Was the relationship draining or did it provide energy for both of you?

5   How effectively were you able to solve problems together?

6   How often did misunderstandings arise and how were they dealt with?

You might have found yourself smiling or grimacing as you thought about your relationship with each person. Take a moment to reflect on what this exercise has clarified for you about the power of relational trust.

Throughout this book, we have argued that the REFRESH characteristics are key to being open to learning. Where relational trust is weak within a team, key aspects of REFRESH will be undermined and huge damage done to the potential for learning. We imagine that the following table will probably tally with some of your reflections in the previous exercise where certain aspects of REFRESH were undermined by low relational trust.

REFRESH characteristic affected	Possible effects of low relational trust
Resilient – willingness to persevere in order to improve your own performance and that of others.	■ Lack of persistence when challenges/setbacks arise. ■ Tendency to externalise blame and ownership for mistakes. ■ Risk of missing development opportunities due to a fear of failing publicly.
Enquiring – showing curiosity about why things are done in a certain way and how they might be done differently.	■ Lack of willingness to pose questions, as there may be doubt about how asking these questions will be perceived. ■ Concern as to whether questions will be listened to and addressed. ■ Doubt about the value of being curious and the amount of energy required. ■ Assumption that any issue is with the question asker, rather than themselves. ■ A tendency to manipulate the enquiries of others to achieve a preferred outcome.
Feedback – exploring which learning gaps have been closed and which remain requires openness to giving and receiving feedback with one another.	■ A defensiveness towards receiving and acting on useful but challenging feedback. ■ A reluctance to provide honest feedback to others for fear of how it will be perceived.

REFRESH characteristic affected	Possible effects of low relational trust
Revising – a willingness to evaluate new knowledge and adapt your existing mental model to it.	■ Closed to new ideas. ■ Resistance to change. ■ A lack of ongoing dialogue about re-evaluating ways of operating. ■ An unconscious bias might exist, such as the halo or horn effects (examined in Chapter 2).
Sharing – learning through collaboration: taking active part in discussions and working to enhance the learning of the whole team.	■ Little sharing of ideas and dialogue. ■ Less collaborative problem solving. ■ A lack of shared clarity.

Given these potential negative elements, it should come as no surprise that low relational trust can be a significant barrier to learning within a team. It is also a reminder of the importance of maintaining high relational trust.

Reflection questions on survey results

On page 53, we offered you a tool to gain feedback from your team on the three barriers to learning. Now is a good time, if you carried out the survey, to reflect on the answers to questions 9–16.

To what extent is low relational trust a barrier to learning in your team?

Which particular issues were flagged up by your team?

Did any aspects of the feedback surprise you?

For questions where the feedback was positive, what has been your contribution to achieving this?

Teams and personnel change over time. It is always a good idea to revisit this survey regularly, perhaps every six months, to see whether the relational trust in your team has developed or not. If you do this, there are three further questions to consider:

How has relational trust improved/deteriorated since the last time the survey was taken?

Why might this be the case?

Are there still persistent relational trust deficits with certain teams and individuals? If so, where and why?

If relational trust is so important to learning, how can leaders nurture and maintain a high trust environment for their team? This question has led us to analyse leaders who have done just that. Although these leaders have many differences in terms of their leadership style and the industries and contexts in which they work, three key common themes emerge: they develop high personal regard for others, they develop high professional regard for others, and they model the qualities of excellent leadership.

These three ingredients have enabled them to create strong communities within their organisations, where everyone feels valued and nurtured both as professionals and as people. The remainder of this chapter provides more details on each of these qualities, as well as some practical strategies to ensure relational trust remains strong.

Developing high personal regard for others

A key influence in shaping the answer to the question, 'Do I trust that person?', will be whether the individual demonstrates personal regard for me. Personal regard refers to whether others treat you as a person worthy of respect and value. It is a basic need for individuals which can sometimes get forgotten in the busy world of work. When personal regard is present, it is typically taken for granted; indeed, it is unusual for individuals to comment on the high level of personal regard in a team. However, when personal regard is missing within a team, it is felt acutely and its absence tends to create dissatisfaction among all. In this section we will explore practical ways to ensure high personal regard doesn't get overlooked and is embedded as a valued norm within the team.

Unconditional positive regard

The phrase 'unconditional positive regard' was coined by the humanist writer and thinker Carl Rogers.[1] He suggested that in order to develop trust with others, it is important to hold them in unconditional positive regard. This requires a basic acceptance of, and respect for, who that person is regardless of what they say or do. For many this can be a huge challenge as it requires us to unconditionally respect others, and to withhold our own preconceptions and judgements about them.

One organisation that was keen to develop personal regard in their workplace invited us to work with their staff to develop a protocol for unconditional positive regard. With our support, the organisation developed a set of very specific protocols and chose to use the following seven behaviours in the workplace:

1   When you talk about any colleague or team member who is not present, do so only in ways that you would feel comfortable with them hearing.

2   When you pass a colleague in the building, smile and acknowledge them.

3   Avoid interrupting others when they are talking.

4   Don't check your phone in meetings or when someone is talking to you.

---

1   Carl Rogers, *Client-Centered Therapy*, 3rd edn (Boston, MA: Houghton Mifflin, 1956).

5   Always say please and thank you when asking a colleague for something.

6   Value others in the same way that you would want to be valued.

7   Be aware of the power that our own negative preconceptions of others can have.

The time invested in developing the protocols paid off. It created a shared language for interpersonal regard. People adopted the protocols and used them; when individuals occasionally forgot they were gently reminded of what they had agreed previously. The training took place in 2008 and the protocols are still in place today. They now form part of the induction training for all new staff and, most importantly, they have transformed the weak relational trust that had existed in the past. They also act as a prompt to avoid unconscious bias against others through our day-to-day behaviours.

The five factor model of personality

Key to building personal regard within a team is to ensure that everyone recognises and accepts that others see the world differently from themselves. As C. S. Lewis wrote, 'For what you see and hear depends a great deal on where you are standing: it also depends on what sort of person you are.'[2] By building this understanding and empathy within a team, we can better anticipate the needs of others and understand how best to work alongside them.

There are many models available to gather insights into personality type, such as the Myers–Briggs Types Indicator (MBTI),[3] DiSC[4] and the Enneagram.[5] Understanding personality type serves several useful purposes in an organisation, including recognising that we are all gifted differently, we all make sense of the world from different perspectives and stages of complexity, and we all get motivated in different and diverse ways. In other words, we don't live in a one-size-fits-all world.

---

2   Clive Staples Lewis, *The Magician's Nephew* (London: Harper Collins Publishers, 1998 [1955]), p. 128.

3   See https://www.myersbriggs.org/my-mbti-personality-type/mbti-basics/home. htm?bhcp=1.

4   See https://www.discprofile.com/what-is-disc/overview.

5   See https://www.enneagraminstitute.com/type-descriptions.

To explore how this is important when developing teams, consider yourself and your team in relation to the five factor (or OCEAN) model.[6] This measures personality against five factors which can be plotted against a continuum running from high to low (see figure on page 94). It is important to realise that wherever an individual sits on the continuum, they have value to add. In other words, there is no right or wrong or best ways to be. Furthermore, many of us can operate across the spectrum through learned behaviours and techniques, but we will relate more deeply and be more energised by certain positions on this continuum. The factors are:

- **Openness.** Individuals who report high openness tend to be adventurous, creative and willing to try new things. Those at the low end tend to prefer existing routines and are likely to be more risk averse. As such they are less comfortable with change, particularly in circumstances where there aren't clear reasons for it.

- **Conscientiousness.** Those who report highly in this factor are usually characterised by their thoroughness and personal organisation. They are likely to be completers/finishers who keep to deadlines rather than get distracted from goals. These individuals prefer to have a set schedule. Those who are low on conscientiousness have a tendency to be more impulsive, finding it harder to conform to routines or structure. As such, they are willing to challenge authority and the status quo, especially when they think there are better alternatives. These individuals tend to prefer more flexible approaches to working.

- **Extraversion.** Individuals high in extraversion tend to be characterised by their outward-going nature. As a result, they are more likely to enjoy meeting new people, as they are conversation starters. They may gain energy from the company of others, as well as being comfortable with being the centre of attention. On occasions, though, these individuals can overlook the risk associated with speaking without thinking. Those who are low in extraversion, on the other hand, tend to be characterised by their reserved nature and more reflective and thoughtful approach. They are likely to consider carefully what they say, and their contributions to discussions are usually well thought out. These individuals are less comfortable in social settings and often have a preference for study and research.

---

6   John M. Digman, 'Personality Structure: Emergence of the Five-Factor Model', *Annual Review of Psychology*, 41(1) (1990), 417–440.

- **Agreeableness.** Kindness, cooperativeness, care and thoughtfulness are characteristics of those who report high in this factor. They tend to show a keen interest in supporting and empathising with others. They place great importance on the feelings of others. Those who score low in this factor are inclined to be more competitive and may lack empathy for others' feelings or problems. This can show itself in being more willing to deliver 'difficult messages' and honest feedback to colleagues when necessary. These individuals are more comfortable with delegating to others.

- **Nervousness.** Those who score highly here may worry about meeting deadlines and hitting targets. This is often due to them being anxious to do the job well. These individuals are apt to anticipate and flag up potential problems and difficulties before they happen. Those at the opposite end of the continuum tend to be more emotionally stable, and are more able to manage stress well. They are less prone to worrying.

By assuming difference rather than similarity (you are different *like me*, rather than you are different *to me*), we can engage in positive curiosity to discover these differences. Understanding the nature of various personalities means individuals are better able to appreciate the impression they convey to others, and why others are different from themselves. They begin to realise how many possibilities exist for conflict, misunderstanding and mistrust – or, alternatively, for high creativity and learning when these differences are harnessed.

When using this model with your team, it is useful to work through a series of stages so individuals can discover which categories best represent them.

Stage 1: Share and unpick the five personality factors

Share each of the different personality factors in turn with your team and talk through the concept of the continuum from high to low for each factor. A useful way to help everyone recognise these personality factors is to consider recognisable workplace examples.

Stage 2: Self-identify

Provide ten minutes or so for each person in the team to self-assess themselves out of 10 for each factor. We have created a free to download self-scoring wheel which graphically demonstrates an individual's scoring pattern. It is available at: www.learningimperative.co.uk/downloads/personality-wheel.

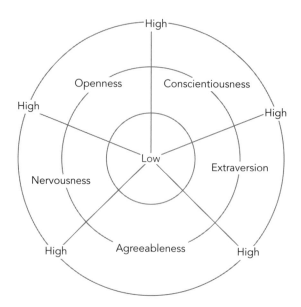

Stage 3: Do others see me as I see myself?

Note: This stage works best by first reminding everyone of the importance of unconditional positive regard, so there is a safe environment for all to talk openly.

Once everyone has self-assessed against the five factors, organise the team into groups of three. Give the groups ten minutes so that everyone can share their self-assessment and get feedback from the rest of the group about whether they see them in the same way. Where there are differences, ask the groups to discuss specific examples of where a particular personality factor has shown itself. For example, one individual might consider themselves to be low on extraversion, and their peers might point to a meeting with a potential customer in which their thoughtful, well-considered contribution played a key role in achieving a successful outcome.

Stage 4: Putting on another's glasses

As a team, move on to examine the potential ways in which a combination of different personalities might create dissonance. Sitting in a circle, share a workplace scenario in which two individuals are at opposite ends of the continuum for a particular personality factor (e.g. openness). Ask the team to 'put on the glasses' of the individual who reports high on the openness continuum: how will this individual view the scenario? Next, ask the team to 'put on the glasses' of the individual who reports low on the openness continuum. It is worth posing the following four questions:

1 How differently does each person view this scenario?

2 How might friction arise between the two of them?

3 How might they frustrate each other if there isn't an appreciation of difference?

4 In what ways does having individuals wearing different glasses enrich our team?

Getting individuals to view the world through the eyes of someone quite different to themselves can be illuminating.

Case study: making time for colleagues

Tim is a leader who, at the outset of our work with him, openly admitted to scoring low on agreeableness. His comment was, 'I haven't got time for small talk at work. I'm not here to socialise.' However, when he examined the personalities of his team, he felt that they were mainly at the opposite end of the continuum. In a follow-up session, he reflected that consciously investing time in conversing with his team on a day-to-day basis had made a massive impact on their morale: 'My team are much more open to me and my ideas for change; they're beginning to see me as a human being.'

Seeing the world through different lenses also enables individuals to realise that they could be projecting their own 'stuff' onto others: seeing others not as they are, but as how they think they are. Seen through our own eyes, our actions seem perfectly normal. But if we look at ourselves through the eyes of others, we might well wish to change some of our behaviours. We may then begin to find that we are better able to see alternative perceptions and possibilities in the way we do things and express ourselves. This was certainly something that Tim, in the last case study, changed straight away with powerful results.

Stage 5: Identifying people's needs

The final stage is to challenge the team to identify the needs of individuals who score in each of the different categories. For example, what are the needs of someone who reports high on the nervousness continuum? How can we work best with that person? What does that person need from us? What examples do the team have of others, at the opposite end of the continuum from themselves, who have made a positive impact? Through this process of deeper understanding of others comes empathy and personal regard.

Reflection question

To what extent are your team a community that demonstrably have high personal regard for one another?

Developing high professional regard for others

Professional regard refers to the extent to which individuals feel valued and supported as employees. When professional regard is strong, individuals feel they are working as part of a community in which there is open and effective communication which aims to develop their KASH. Our experience from working with organisations where professional regard is recognised by staff as a strength is that the following elements need to be in place: avoiding processing overload; recognising individual improvement; opportunities for growth and development; and communication that inspires trust.

Reducing processing overload

In Chapter 3, we described the barriers to learning that processing overload and a lack of shared clarity can present. A crucial aspect of demonstrating professional regard for others is habitually seeking to avoid overloading individuals with the stressful experience of feeling overwhelmed by too much information.

Some years ago, we worked with a leadership team operating in a busy work environment with whom we collaboratively developed a neat approach. Now, whenever they evaluate new strategies, they always challenge themselves to consider the processing load implications of their choices and decisions. If the new strategy is going to lead to more work for the team, they ask themselves: what are we going to ask the team to stop doing in order to make time for it? These reflections have led them to be more careful in implementing change, as well as creating a valuable opportunity to monitor and evaluate the effectiveness of the team. One question they frequently ask is: how can we get to a better outcome by continuously improving the process?

Noticing and recognising improvement in others

In fast paced work environments, where there is a constant focus on improvement and targets, the personal growth of individuals can go unnoticed – and with it, a key ingredient for establishing high professional regard.

In our analysis, leaders who create environments of high relational trust tend to maintain a habitual focus on, and recognition of, improvements in the performance of colleagues. One leader put it succinctly when she said, 'My job isn't only to constantly focus on spotting gaps in the team's performance; it's to notice the efforts people have put in to narrow the gaps too.' Employees' resentment towards, and sense of disconnect from, colleagues and managers whose recognition of individual improvement is missing can lead to frustration, resistance and withdrawal. Above all, a recognition of progress affirms that the behaviours that everyone is seeking to encourage and put in place are reinforced.

For some leaders, this ability to notice and recognise team members' contributions is a well-developed habit. For others, it makes sense to add it to their kanban chart and embed it as a desired and desirable behaviour.

Case study: the power of noticing

'It put a big smile on my face on Saturday morning.' This was the reaction of Jane, who had received a thank you card through the post from her team leader. It was for her actions the previous week when she had de-escalated a potentially difficult incident with an aggressive customer. This thank you card wasn't a one-off. It was the norm for this leader. He understood the importance of demonstrating professional regard by noticing and recognising the efforts of his team in delivering excellent service. His team certainly valued it because every staff survey showed that their high performance was recognised.

It can be a card in the post, the regular nomination of a team member of the week or a quiet, reflective thank you over coffee. Whatever it is, the power of noticing and appreciating good work can go a very long way towards building trust.

Providing effective opportunities for growth and development

Crucial to building professional regard in the team is ensuring that colleagues have access to opportunities for professional learning that effectively meet their needs. In Part III, we provide a clear and detailed methodology with which to design and deliver effective learning. However, opportunities for learning and development need not only be formal learning programmes; much professional learning takes place on a day-to-day basis in meetings and discussions within teams. Indeed, in Chapter 3, we showed ways in which effective dialogue and reflection can be part of the everyday habits of a high achieving learning team.

Communication that inspires trust

Building relational trust is a lot like the tower-building game, Jenga. It can take a long time to build, but it can be completely destroyed in a thoughtless moment. For this reason, it is good to bear in mind that there are two complementary sides to effective two-way communication: how well you talk and how well you listen.

Here are some ideas that can help you to communicate more effectively and build professional respect without damaging personal relationships. Of course, you might think you already communicate well, but the results of the survey questions in Appendix 1 will help you to explore how valid your perception actually is.

Straight talking

Straight talking means being clear about your internal thinking processes and dialogue, and making it transparent to others so they know where you are coming from. So ask yourself: what am I noticing? What ideas do I have? What am I feeling? What assumptions am I making? And then share these insights explicitly and transparently with colleagues and co-workers. Turn your inner chatter into clear conversation so others don't have to mind-read. When your communication is direct, other people's light bulbs go on as they begin to understand your viewpoint. Invite others to use these same steps when they communicate with you (and others) in one-to-ones and in meetings.

When straight talking is explicitly introduced and modelled by the team leader, and then adopted by everyone else, it can blow away many hidden agendas and allow everyone to talk openly and freely about their ideas and enthusiasms, their concerns and anxieties. In particular, it encourages an adult-to-adult mode of communication, which sets aside status and experience, while avoiding the pitfalls of the parent–child style of leadership. It enhances independent thought and responsibility and diminishes dependency and passive-aggressive resistance.

It is essential to promote a culture in which team members are confident that their input, challenges and alternative perspectives (whether you agree with them or not) are seen as creative contributions to valuable learning and change, not as dissent or disrespect. Techniques such as straight talking enable everyone to express themselves with directness without appearing rude or overly forceful.

Behavioural feedback

Encourage everyone to give feedback on behaviour, not identity, and model this yourself. What does this mean? If someone says to you: 'You're a great presenter' (identity), it is nice to hear but utterly unhelpful. If they were to say, 'I liked the way you gave me level eye contact; it made me feel connected to you,' you know exactly what behaviour they appreciated and what to continue working on. Separate behaviour from identity, just as you might say to a child, 'I love you but I don't like it when you do X.'

When giving behavioural feedback, it is also valuable to express your emotional response and add an additional suggestion, whether your feedback is favourable or challenging. Here is a useful equation to use in these circumstances: 'When you X [behaviour], it makes me feel Y [emotion], and what I'd suggest/prefer is Z [additional or different behaviour].' For example:

- 'When you ask for feedback on your performance [behaviour], it makes me feel excited [emotion] that you are open to feedback, and what I suggest is that you try these (specific) strategies [additional or different behaviour].'

- 'When you don't ask for feedback [behaviour], it makes me feel anxious [emotion] that you are not keen to develop your performance skills, and what I'd prefer is that we agree to meet weekly on Tuesdays at 10 a.m. to see how things are going [additional or different behaviour].'

These interventions are best concluded by asking the other person for their take on your feedback. There is more on how to create a high quality feedback environment in Chapter 5.

Active listening

There are various ways to model active listening: take notes, ask questions to get clarification, paraphrase what has been said to check meaning and understanding, listen before you speak, and avoid interrupting unless absolutely necessary. If a speaker is not communicating clearly, gently ask them to summarise their thoughts – for instance, 'Could you say again what your top three issues are?' or 'Can you summarise that in a nutshell, please?'

Active listening is one of the most powerful and elegant ways to demonstrate personal and professional respect.

Here is an active listening exercise to try with colleagues:

1   Work in pairs (A and B).

2   Ask B's to leave the room and wait outside.

3   Tell the A's they are going to listen to the B's for ninety seconds. They should listen actively for the first thirty seconds, then gradually and deliberately lose interest for the next thirty seconds, and then re-establish excellent listening for the last thirty seconds.

4   Outside the room, tell the B's to identify something positive they have experienced during the last six months. They will have ninety seconds to talk about it with their partner A.

5   Invite the B's back into the room and start the pairs off all at the same time.

6   At the end of the ninety seconds, ask the B's how they felt when the A's listening behaviour changed.

7   Ask both A's and B's to compile a checklist for active listening.

We have always found this to be a useful training exercise. In a very short amount of time, everyone gets to appreciate the difference between good listening and poor listening and to co-create a list of success criteria for active listening.

Both straight talking and active listening improve relational trust. They open pathways for honest, open and transparent communication, they save time and they ensure that everyone can say their piece and be heard respectfully.

The importance of leadership modelling

We will now consider the final aspect of building higher relational trust: boosting your personal and professional credibility through modelling the qualities that will build strong relational trust with others.

The way that others perceive our level of credibility will influence how far they are likely to offer us their trust. People ask themselves, 'Is that person's advice worth listening to?' or 'Is their analysis of the way forward a useful one for me to adopt?' There is a lot of sense to this because the success of our own career may well be determined by our ability to recognise competence in others, so we need to ask the right questions of the right people.

How well, or not, you are rated as a leader by your peers and your team will likely depend on the credibility and trust you develop through your ability to deliver across all aspects of your professional role. Indeed, competence and trust are inseparable. As Professor David DeSteno, author of *The Truth About Trust*, argues, 'Even if everyone likes you, you have to be competent to be trusted.'[7] This is the final fundamental ingredient in the relational trust glue for any team.

Case study: modelling – it's a full-time job!

Jim, a leader we worked with for some years, had a great question when coaching budding leaders in his organisation. He asked them, 'What message did your actions and your body language send out in addition to what you said?' He wanted to challenge those he was coaching to reflect on how being a model for others requires paying attention to every aspect of what they say and do. It is not a part-time job. It is something we are doing all the time, whether we like it or not!

Beyond personal and professional regard for others, what are the fundamental qualities of relational trust that we need to build into our leadership modelling? We love the personal affirmation a leader shared with us over coffee at a conference in London. We were discussing relational trust and this prompted her to pull from her suit pocket what appeared to be a business card. In fact, it was a pledge that she had printed to remind herself how important it was to be a leadership role model. She told us that whenever someone in her team left to take up a leadership post of their own, she would give them a copy of her pledge.

---

7   Quoted in Carolyn O'Hara, 'Proven Ways to Earn Your Employees' Trust', *Harvard Business Review* (27 June 2014). Available at: https://hbr.org/2014/06/proven-ways-to-earn-your-employees-trust.

The card reminded her of the necessity of modelling excellent leadership continually and transparently, right across the business – with the receptionist on the front desk, with her team in formal and informal meetings, with senior leaders, with customers and with clients.

Her card got us thinking about creating a list of our own, based on our experience and research and our observation of excellent leaders who generate high levels of trust. We invite you to create a pledge card of your own, drawing from the following principles.

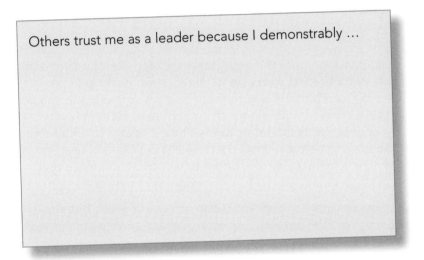

Others trust me as a leader because I demonstrably …

Showing integrity

Integrity is demonstrated through honesty, moral judgement and character. Leaders who build high levels of trust demonstrate that they understand right from wrong, which guides all their actions including decision making and the way they conduct their relationships – for example, they are open and authentic, and don't hide information or operate hidden agendas. A good test of your own integrity is to challenge your own behaviours by asking: would I find it fair to be treated this way myself?

Righting any wrongs

From time to time leaders make mistakes. When mistakes are made, high trust leaders know the importance of demonstrating humility by acknowledging them, apologising quickly and repairing any ill-will caused. These leaders understand that the negative consequences of trying to cover it up, or blaming others for it, are profound.

Keeping commitments

High trust leaders recognise the importance of keeping their commitments. This involves two steps: the first step is to be clear on what you are committing to do, and the second step is to make sure that you do it. Some leaders need to guard against making promises in the heat of the moment, especially when addressing immediate concerns. It is far better to take time out and consider more carefully whether the commitment you intend to make is deliverable. Over-promising and not delivering is a perfect way to erode the trust and confidence that others have in you.

Keeping commitments not only applies to achieving goals, but also to confidentiality: keeping confidences and respecting others' private concerns.

Showing loyalty to others

The leader who builds high levels of trust knows the importance of demonstrating support and personal and professional regard for individuals and for the team – for example, this might include giving credit for operational success to the team rather than yourself. The same applies to moments when things go less well. When things go awry, the team leader should be the first person to put their hand up and take responsibility, thereby shielding their team (of course, some straight talking may occur later in private).

Many of the principles that we discussed in the earlier section on unconditional positive regard apply to the modelling of loyalty – in particular, talking behind people's backs should be strenuously avoided. On the other hand, making sure team members are invited and encouraged to put forward opposing and challenging views is a great way to build a cohesive team culture. For example, 'I think Sue might have different views on this issue. It would probably be much more productive to have that conversation as soon as possible, and with her present,' demonstrates this leader's loyalty to Sue and his support of her right to uphold contradictory views.

Demonstrating a passion for excellence

The high trust leader models a passion for excellence rather than what is just OK. On a day-to-day basis, they bring an intellectual, emotional and physical energy towards improvement and development within the team. From time to time, of course, straight talking will be necessary to tackle problems that may arise – and the high trust leader invites straight talking in both directions.

Overall, the willingness of a leader to meet challenges and issues head-on, rather than skirting around them or turning a blind eye, will raise the leader's profile in the team's estimation. This is an area we will examine in greater depth in Chapter 5.

Showing a commitment to getting better

A leader who builds high trust commits, on a continuing basis, to develop their own KASH through their openness to learning, and ensures that this is visible to the team. This commitment may be driven by many reasons – for instance, a recognition that their current KASH may not be sufficient to meet the challenges of a rapidly changing and complex future, because through learning they avoid becoming complacent and stale or because they wish to show a good example to their team.

This commitment to learning will likely include seeking deeper insights into the effectiveness of their own leadership, eliciting timely and developmental feedback from others, and carving out time for self-reflection. We find that these leaders have an insatiable desire to constantly deepen their capacities and widen their horizons. In other words, they are asking themselves whether they are a better version of themselves than they were three, six or nine months ago. They are also enquiring into what kind of leader and model they might become in the months and years ahead.

Reflection questions

How far do you agree with David DeSteno's quote about the need to be 'competent to be trusted'?

Which qualities of leadership modelling do you identify as being your own natural habits, and which ones are not? What do you plan to do about it?

The goal of achieving high relational trust within a team is both challenging and potentially hugely rewarding. The challenge lies in the need for all members of the team, including the leader, to discipline themselves to a way of working and interacting that aligns with the personal and professional regard of others. The reward lies in creating a team where trust acts as a wonderfully strong glue which holds the team together, regardless of what change, innovation or disturbance brings.

Maintaining strong relational trust action plan
What could be the start/stop actions in terms of creating high personal regard within your team?
What could be the start/stop actions in terms of creating high professional regard within your team?
What could be the start/stop actions in terms of modelling leadership excellence within your team?

Start actions

Stop actions

REFRESH reading list

Some suggested reading if you want to delve deeper:

Achor, Shawn (2010). *The Happiness Advantage: How a Positive Brain Fuels Success in Work and Life* (New York: Crown Business).

Covey, Stephen M. R. and Merrill, Rebecca (2006). *The Speed of Trust: The One Thing That Changes Everything* (New York: Simon & Schuster).

Goleman, Daniel (2004). *Emotional Intelligence and Working with Emotional Intelligence* (London: Bloomsbury).

Maister, David, Galford, Robert and Green, Charles (2002). *The Trusted Advisor* (London: Simon & Schuster).

Radcliffe, Steve (2012). *Leadership: Plain and Simple*, 2nd edn (Harlow: Pearson Education).

Schein, Edgar H. (2011). *Helping: How to Offer, Give, and Receive Help* (San Francisco, CA: Berrett-Koehler).

Schein, Edgar H. (2013). *Humble Inquiry: The Gentle Art of Asking Instead of Telling* (San Francisco, CA: Berrett-Koehler).

Chapter 5

Perception gaps

In 1995, McArthur Wheeler robbed two Pittsburgh banks in broad daylight. Not only did he do so without any attempt to disguise himself, but he actually smiled at the surveillance cameras as he walked out of each bank. Later that night, to his genuine surprise, police arrested him at his home. When they showed him the banks' surveillance tapes, Wheeler stared in disbelief. 'But I wore the juice,' he exclaimed. Wheeler thought that rubbing lemon juice onto his skin would render him invisible to videotape cameras. His logic was that lemon juice can be used as invisible ink on paper. As long as he didn't go near a heat source, so his thinking went, he should have been completely invisible.

Wheeler is an extreme example of something all of us suffer from to varying degrees: delusion. Our preferred name for such delusions is 'perception gaps'. A perception gap is the difference between how a person perceives his or her current performance or potential compared with the reality of the situation. In the workplace they mainly occur in three particular ways: some perceive their work performance to be better than it really is, others perceive that it is worse than it actually is, and some perceive that their performance cannot improve.

■ Have you ever led or managed anyone who grossly overestimated their performance?

■ Is there anyone in your team who believes they don't need to improve?

■ Are there members of your team who hold limiting beliefs about themselves which prevent them from improving?

If the answer to any of these questions is yes, then this chapter will give you information and strategies to help you close these gaps.

What's in this chapter for me?

This chapter will help you to diagnose perception gaps in your team using real-life examples from different types of organisations. We will explain how and why these gaps arise and how to address them. We will also offer some practical strategies to reduce or eliminate the perception gaps to prevent them occurring again.

Why does this matter? Our experience suggests that if these perception gaps are not addressed then your team's performance will, at best, stay exactly where it is, or, at worst, deteriorate.

Before continuing, remind yourself of where you plotted the positions of your team members on the learning–performance matrix, bearing in mind the effects of the halo effect and the horn effect (see Chapter 2).

Types of perception gap

We have identified four types of perception gap that exist in the workplace. Each one is different but they all act as barriers to becoming a better performer. We will describe each of them with reference to the learning–performance matrix.

The first two perception gaps pertain to individuals who *overestimate* their performance or how open they are to learning. Psychologists David Dunning and Justin Kruger of Cornell University, who studied the failed bank robber case, concluded that some people mistakenly assess their abilities as being much higher than they actually are. This illusion of confidence is called the 'Dunning–Kruger effect', and describes how those most lacking in knowledge and skills are the least able to appreciate that lack.[1] Overestimating our competence (or self-enhancement) at work or in other situations is not a new phenomenon. It has probably been around since the dawn of humankind. False perceptions around

---

1   Justin Kruger and David Dunning, 'Unskilled and Unaware of It: How Difficulties in Recognizing One's Own Incompetence Lead to Inflated Self-Assessments', *Journal of Personality and Social Psychology*, 77(6) (1999), 1121–1134.

performance are common. In August 2007, *BusinessWeek* surveyed 2,000 Americans in middle management positions and above, asking them the question, 'Are you one of the top 10% of performers in your company?' More than 80% of the respondents, covering every subgroup in the survey, answered the question affirmatively; 84% of all middle managers reported that they were in the top 10% of performers in their company. Among senior executives – the most deluded cluster by far – 97% of those who were asked whether they were in the top 10% answered yes.[2]

According to Dunning and Kruger: 'When people are incompetent in the strategies they adopt to achieve success and satisfaction, they suffer a dual burden: not only do they reach erroneous conclusions and make unfortunate choices, but their incompetence robs them of the ability to realize it.'[3] And there's more bad news. Even when incompetent individuals are taught about the false superiority that accompanies self-enhancement, many of them believe that it applies to others and not to them. This is why the Dunning–Kruger effect is also known as the 'dumb and dumber effect'.[4] Their self-rating around work performance is much higher than is borne out by reality, and they also struggle to recognise their relatively low levels of competence when compared to real high performers.

The other two perception gaps relate to individuals who *underestimate* how good they are in their role or think they are incapable of learning to be a better performer. These perception gaps are sometimes referred to as 'imposter syndrome' because these individuals doubt their own performance and have a persistent fear of being outed as a low performer. For many suffering from this limiting belief, the notion of being a high performer or the possibility of becoming a high performer is disregarded.

Perception gap 1: Overestimating performance

Liam rates himself as a very effective deputy store manager and is beginning to apply for store manager positions. He couldn't be a friendlier or more helpful

---

2   See Dick Grote, 'Let's Abolish Self-Appraisal', *Harvard Business Review* (11 July 2011). Available at: https://hbr.org/2011/07/lets-abolish-self-appraisal.
3   Kruger and Dunning 'Unskilled and Unaware of It', at. 1121.
4   John Hattie and Gregory C. R. Yates, *Visible Learning and the Science of How We Learn* (Abingdon: Routledge, 2014), p. 233.

colleague. He always remembers people's birthdays and has boundless enthusiasm for improving the morale of his staff. In his role, he perceives himself to be a high performer. In reality he is anything but. Liam is at his best when he is interacting with colleagues, but on the crucial administration and recording aspects of his job, he is not good at all. But he is blind to these flaws or sees them as only a minor, less important part of the job compared to building relationships. Liam overinflates this part of his KASH to such an extent that it completely overshadows all other aspects. He often messes up staffing rotas and is frequently late when supplying critical information to his superiors.

In a recent staff review, when asked to rate his overall effectiveness, Liam's self-rating averaged out at around 9 out of 10. The area manager, who has nine years of extensive experience managing and overseeing stores, using more objective measures, gave him a 4! Quite a gap.

Let's revisit the learning–performance matrix to explain this type of perception gap in more detail:

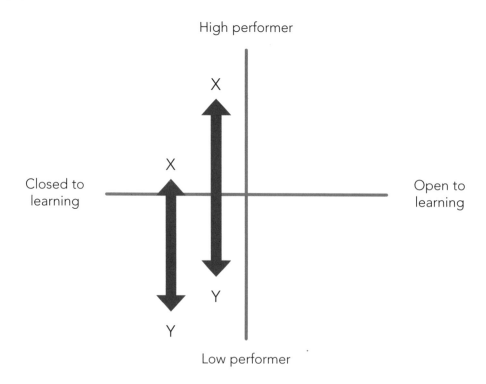

Using the learning–performance matrix we used in Chapter 2, X stands for the individual's self-rating, whereas Y is the reality. We have placed two individuals within the matrix, both of whom suffer from the Dunning–Kruger effect. Each has a different sized perception gap. The arrow on the left represents an individual who rates his performance as average. However, in reality, he is a low performer at point Y. The second perception gap is even larger and represents someone who is a low performer but actually sees themselves as a high performer. This could easily represent someone like Liam in the case history above.

When you use the matrix to plot your team's performance, your assessment may well be different from theirs. Those who suffer from this perception gap are likely to be under the illusion that they don't need to be open to learning because their level of performance is already good enough. Although *you* may want your colleagues to improve, *they* will perceive that they don't need to make any changes. Sure, they may participate in dialogue about improvement and development, but they are unlikely to engage with it fully because they consider it to be unnecessary. From their perspective, they are already performing well.

Perception gap 2:
Overestimating openness to learning

In Chapter 2 we introduced the REFRESH acronym. This describes how people who are open to learning are resilient, enquiring, feedback-craving, revising, effort-making sharers who possess habits that help them to learn effectively. Those who overestimate their openness to learning have fallen into the trap of perceiving that they demonstrate more of the REFRESH characteristics than they actually do.

Louise sees herself as a good saleswoman and a good learner. However, she is also pretty stubborn – and when she's right, she's right. When it comes to her annual performance review, Louise grudgingly participates. What is holding her back from being a better performer is her mental model. Colleagues with a better track record regard her work practices as inefficient, but she is comfortable with the way she does things. She is happy to tweak what she does, but in reality what she needs is a complete transformation. One example of this is Louise's dogged refusal to adopt some of the techniques that high performers use. She even shadowed someone for a few days to learn their methods, but from Louise's perspective these methods don't appear to be much different from her own.

Both individuals represented in the diagram below have different gaps – point X represents their perceived openness to learning and point Y represents where they actually are. Both individuals represented here suffer from the Dunning–Kruger effect, but this time it is around how open to learning they are.

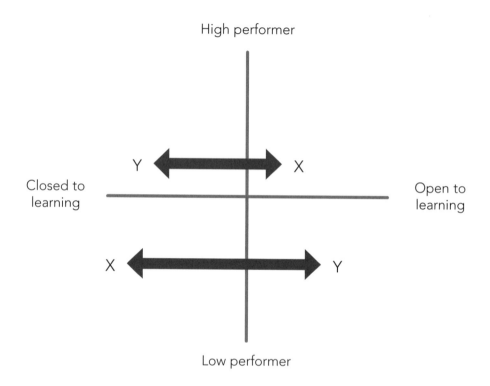

We can again utilise the REFRESH model, using the revising characteristic as a reference point. We define revising as a willingness to evaluate new knowledge and adapt your existing mental model to take account of it. Team members with stuck mental models may think they are revisers even when they are not. Authentic revisers will always be willing to adapt their beliefs and viewpoints in the light of compelling new evidence. Louise might think she is open to learning but she is deluding herself. Whenever she comes across new information, she fits it into her existing model and applies what is known in the trade as 'confirmation bias'.[5] In other words, she tends to discard any new information, data or evidence that does not fit her existing mental model.

Team leaders and supervisors who are unaware of these two types of perception gap can waste huge amounts of time and energy designing learning experiences that are doomed to fail. These types of perception gap mean it is unlikely that you will coax any improved performance from these individuals.

Causes of the Dunning–Kruger effect

Liam and Louise represent individuals who rate their performance and attitude to learning respectively as being higher than is warranted. There may be various reasons for this. Wheeler misunderstood the power of lemon juice. In preparation for the robberies, he smeared his face with lemon juice and took a Polaroid photo to see if it worked. When the picture was developed he could not identify himself. He therefore concluded, from this single source of evidence, that lemon juice had the power to make him invisible. He discarded the possibilities that the camera or film were faulty, that the picture was over-exposed or that the lemon juice was blurring his vision! If he had been open to learning – for instance, using more sources of feedback, more data, and taking more time to reflect – he could have avoided twenty-six years in prison.

Wheeler became deluded because of two things: lack of effective feedback and an overinflated sense of his own brilliance. The combination of these two factors are often at play when the Dunning–Kruger effect arises.

All of us have an ego. It can be a help or a hindrance to becoming a better learner. An overinflated ego can hold us back from being better learners and consequently better performers. Individuals with overly large egos are particularly prone to overrating their performance levels. They rarely see the value in reflecting more deeply or taking feedback from others. The notion of an inflated sense of ego is beautifully captured in the story of 'The Emperor's New Clothes'. Only a young child, who can still see clearly and is unafraid of looking foolish, states the naked truth: the Emperor isn't wearing anything at all! But the Emperor, caught up in his puffed up self-image, continues his progress through the town.

---

5   See Scott Plous, *The Psychology of Judgment and Decision Making* (Columbus, OH: McGraw-Hill Education, 1993), p. 233.

The tale warns against being too full of your own abilities and having delusions of grandeur.

In their 2003 paper 'Why People Fail to Recognize Their Own Incompetence', Dunning and Kruger assert that incorrect self-rating of work performance mostly derives from the person's ignorance of, or confusion about, the performance standards required for that job or task.[6] We need to ask three questions here:

1   Have the key performance indicators been clearly explained?

2   Are the assessment systems fit for purpose?

3   Is feedback given in a helpful way?

In our experience, flawed feedback processes and a lack of clarity about best practice are likely to be major reasons why people lack awareness about their real performance abilities.

A particular feedback issue is rater bias. This occurs when managers withhold tough but necessary feedback because they fear jeopardising their relationship with a team member. We are also aware of many situations in which team leaders have not pulled their punches and instead offered feedback that is not only worse than useless, but contributes to the employees' continuing sense of their own high worth.

Reflection questions

Who in your team might be overestimating the level of their performance?

What symptoms do they display that suggest this?

6   David Dunning, Kerri Johnson, Joyce Ehrlinger and Justin Kruger, 'Why People Fail to Recognize Their Own Incompetence', *Current Directions in Psychological Science*, 12(3) (2003), 83–87.

What are the effects of this perception gap on their openness to learning?

In each case, what do you think has caused the Dunning–Kruger effect: lack of clarity, overconfidence, feedback issues or a combination of these?

The other two perception gaps fall under the category of imposter syndrome, whereby individuals underestimate themselves and doubt their own performance. Indeed, they will go so far as to attribute any isolated success to luck or to others. Unfortunately, this means they are more likely to lack self-confidence and underestimate their potential.

Perception gap 3: Underestimating performance

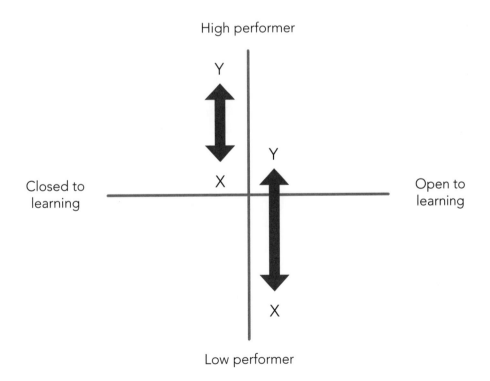

Ian works in sales, working on his own on the road much of the time. As a result, he doesn't get much opportunity to see the work of his peers. Being the perfectionist that he is, Ian often beats himself up for not being good at all aspects of his job. He is not great at networking, and, being an introvert, Ian is not as comfortable in establishing relationships with potential new customers as some of his other colleagues are. Nevertheless, when it comes to actual performance, Ian excels in key areas. The problem is that he overly focuses on his limitations and not his strengths. He is a classic example of someone whose self-rating is much lower on the vertical performance axis than it should be.

Both individuals represented within the matrix on page 117 have different sized perception gaps. As before, X represents the individual's self-rating, whereas Y is the reality. The person on the left perceives their performance as being just above average when in fact it is much higher. This could be someone like Ian. The one on the right reflects someone who believes they are a low performer when in reality they are above average. Might these reflect members of your team?

Many people who underestimate their performance level are likely to lack confidence. They will plot themselves at a lower position on the learning–performance matrix than others would. Their uncertainty around performance issues may also mean that they are more stressed than they need to be, often worrying about things unnecessarily. Their processing space is taken up by being anxious about things they can already do, thereby diminishing opportunities for learning new things that could help them to thrive. The good news is that you have a great opportunity to develop their performance and openness to learning by realigning their perception with reality.

Perception gap 4: Underestimating potential

Vincent always looked forward to meeting a new team for the first time. Having worked in the hospitality industry for over thirty years, he had built up vast experience. He had forgotten the number of times he had given these introductory talks when taking over the management of a new bar or hotel, and these sessions had always gone well – setting the vision for the team and how they were going to be successful, getting to know the staff, creating that important positive first impression. Once again it seemed to have gone well.

Later in the day, he was looking through a bundle of staff questionnaires that he had asked everyone to complete. There was one that really stood out. To the question: 'How do you rate your level of performance in your current role?', Steve had written: 'I'd rate myself as average. I don't think I can ever be a high performer.' On further investigation, Vincent found that Steve had worked at the hotel for twelve years and over that time he had become increasingly closed to learning. For Vincent to succeed in his new role, he would need everybody to up their game. He was faced with the challenge of trying to get Steve to see that his negative perception about improvement was just plain wrong.

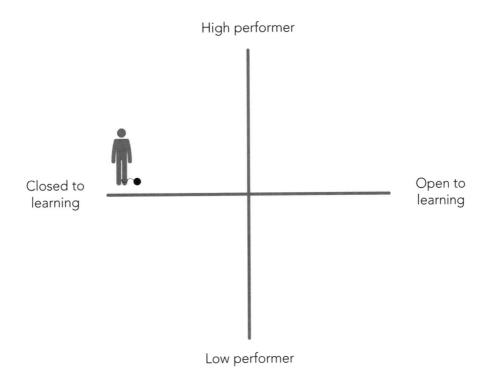

On this learning–performance matrix there are no arrows. Instead, there is a figure tied to a ball and chain. It represents this individual's perception that improvement is impossible. In this case, the person's performance is just above average.

People who have a negative idea of their potential have developed limiting beliefs about themselves. Of course, not everyone is capable of being in the top 1% of performers, but from our experience, we would argue passionately that everyone can learn to become a better performer than they are currently. But the chances of this happening are massively reduced if an individual's self-belief is that improvement is impossible.

Causes of imposter syndrome

The causes of imposter syndrome are our old friends ego and feedback, but in quite different ways than before.

Some individuals in organisations have insufficiently developed egos. They lack the psychological maturity and confidence to believe that they can ever be high performers. Each of us holds different beliefs or models of reality – because our senses filter information differently, one person can perceive an experience or event in a quite different way to someone else. People whose egos are insufficiently resilient tend to filter out their successful individual contributions. Instead, they look for evidence that reinforces their disempowering beliefs that they are not a good performer and are incapable of becoming one in the future.

Just as ineffective feedback can be a contributory cause of the Dunning–Kruger effect, imposter syndrome can arise for exactly the same reasons. For example, when the feedback an individual receives on their performance is unduly critical, or the guidance is vague or contradictory, or where the step change advice is poor or missing, it is no surprise that he or she is at risk of developing imposter syndrome. Similarly, the complete absence of feedback from others about their performance can mean that individuals don't recognise the value they add. In certain organisations, this syndrome seems to spread like a virus among staff due to ineffective or inappropriate feedback.

Reflection questions

Who in your team might be suffering from perception gaps caused by a lack of self-belief?

What symptoms do they display that suggest this?

What are the effects of their perception gap on their openness to learning?

What might have caused imposter syndrome to arise in each particular team member – lack of confidence or feedback issues?

Do you have any individuals who, like Ian, are held back because they don't realise their true level of performance?

Are there any individuals in your team who don't perceive that they have the capacity to develop?

Reflection questions on survey

On page 53, we offered you a tool to gain feedback from your team on the three barriers to learning. Now is a good time, if you carried out the survey, to reflect on the answers to questions 17–22.

To what extent are perception gaps a barrier to learning in your team?

Were there any particular issues that were flagged up by your team?

Did any aspects of the feedback surprise you?

For questions to which feedback was positive, what has been your own contribution to achieving this?

Strategies to reduce perception gaps

Why are we confident that these perception gaps can be closed? We know because organisations we have worked with have efficiently closed these gaps by using the techniques we are advocating. Indeed, we have worked with leaders who have been very effective in creating a culture where perception and reality have become inseparable buddies. After all, it is surely much better to establish an environment in which perception gaps are eradicated than having to continually deal with their effects on learning and performance. Of course, there are extremes – for example, those rare individuals who are struggling with extreme narcissism or low self-esteem where the issues run far deeper. But in our experience, most individuals can be supported to close their perception gaps.

Key to the successful taming of perception gaps is the creation of feedback environments that ensure individuals are crystal clear about best practice and their personal impact on its delivery. In the two preceding chapters, we have examined strategies to reduce processing overload and strengthen relational trust. Fortuitously, these strategies are the foundations for effective feedback within a team.

In Chapter 3, you will recall that we focused on the importance of generating shared clarity. High quality feedback depends on having shared clarity not just about expectations, but also on what beautiful looks and sounds like, as well as clarity about the process of getting there. Therefore, for those seeking to close perception gaps within their team, it is imperative that they create a shared language for excellence, and that there is ongoing dialogue and reflection about this. Unless there is a common language and a mutual understanding about what excellence is, then the quality of feedback is invariably poor.

In Chapter 4, we examined strategies designed to elicit strong relational trust. Relational trust supports everyone involved in the feedback process to feel more able to be open and honest without fear of misunderstanding or misrepresentation.

Trust allows a robust and open exchange of views with opportunities for clarification. In our experience, where relational trust is strong there is less chance that critical feedback is taken personally; instead, it is perceived as an opportunity to improve and develop. At the same time, those whose job it is to give feedback feel much more comfortable doing so, even with sensitive issues, as they are less likely to encounter defensiveness.

For the remainder of this chapter, we will examine strategies that utilise this high clarity–high trust environment in order to ensure that feedback creates an accurate perception of performance within the team. There are two sources of feedback that inform our view of the world around us: the feedback we give ourselves and the feedback we get from others.

Self-feedback

Self-feedback on our own performance happens on a continual basis. It is the source of the vast majority of feedback that is available to us, although we may not always give it our full attention. Basically, we are evaluating whether we are on the right track to achieve what we perceive to be a decent outcome. For many routine and mundane tasks, such as making a cup of tea, this happens on an unconscious level. We make judgements about whether the tea has brewed for long enough and whether we have put sufficient milk in the cup.

In order to develop the quality of feedback we give ourselves, there are two key elements which require our focus and attention. First, we need to slow down our thinking so we can assess whether the feedback we are giving ourselves is accurate. In many cases, where perception gaps exist, we may be unwittingly ignoring important information that would radically reshape our self-feedback. On the pages that follow, we will examine two strategies proven to slow down thinking within a team: (1) reducing inattentional blindness using the 'ladder of inference', and (2) video analysis.

The second element is to ensure that clarity about best practice is freely available to the team so everyone has a clear barometer to calibrate their own perception of high performance. In order to achieve this, we will describe ways to make quality work publicly available.

Regardless of the causes of whatever perception gaps individuals may hold, getting them to be more self-aware is crucial to improving the quality of the feedback they are able to give themselves. Consequently, the strategies in this section will help to overcome perception gaps caused by the Dunning–Kruger effect and imposter syndrome.

Reducing inattentional blindness using the ladder of inference

One of the unwelcome consequences of processing overload is the way it can lead to the incorrect filtering of information. This problem can play a key role in creating what is known as 'inattentional blindness', a quality which not only leads us to see precisely what we are expecting to see, but also affects how we make judgements based on this blinkered information.[7] Daniel Kahneman, in his book *Thinking, Fast and Slow*, refers to this when he writes, 'we can be blind to the obvious, and we are also blind to our blindness'.[8] Time and again in our work with organisations, overcoming inattentional blindness – through the application of effective strategies – has been crucial to closing perception gaps. Once this is achieved, not only do teams become better at noticing the things they have previously failed to notice, but they also notice how this failing has affected their perception of performance.

The ladder of inference is a great tool for reducing inattentional blindness and can be used by both individuals and teams. First developed by organisational psychologist Chris Argyris, the ladder of inference sets out the thinking steps we go through, usually unconsciously, to get to a decision or action. The ladder can be used to slow down and question each thinking step, one at a time, to ensure that inattentional blindness is not unwittingly leading us to form inaccurate judgements about the world around us.[9]

---

7   See Arien Mack and Irvin Rock, *Inattentional Blindness* (Cambridge, MA: MIT Press, 1998).

8   Kahneman, *Thinking, Fast and Slow*, p. 32.

9   The figure has been adapted from Peter Senge, Art Kleiner, Charlotte Roberts, Richard B. Ross and Bryan Smith, *The Fifth Discipline Fieldbook: Strategies and Tools for Building a Learning Organization* (London: Nicholas Brealey, 2010 [1994]), pp. 242–246.

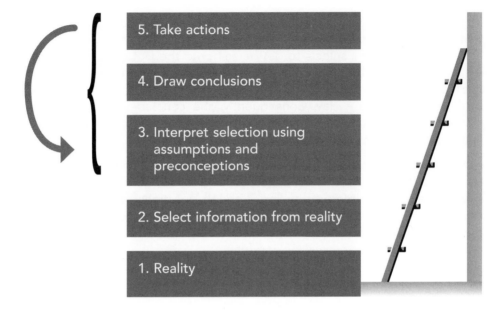

The ladder of inference works in the following way:

Rung 1: The environment around us (reality) provides a limitless pool of information from which to draw.

Rung 2: The individual (or team) selects from the available information – a little like drawing a bucket of water from a pool. Selection happens because no individual has the capacity to process all of the available information. The quality of our selection is what is important here. Selection, as we have seen above, is often guided by what someone expects to see in a given situation, rather than other factors that might improve it.

Rung 3: The individual (or team) interprets the information they have selected in order to give it meaning. This interpretation is often influenced by existing assumptions, unconscious bias or preconceptions.

Rung 4: Once the information has been interpreted, the individual (or team) draws conclusions or judgements based upon their interpretation.

Rung 5: The individual (or team) decides what actions to take based on their conclusions.

This is how the ladder of inference works in practice: in a meeting, Marie observes that Calvin seems to be quieter than usual and is not offering her eye contact. This is the data Marie selects to get herself onto the first rung. Next, she adds meaning to these observations and assumes that Calvin is upset with her. From this Marie concludes that Calvin is probably sulking because of a critical email she sent him the previous day. Consequently, she concludes that Calvin is thin-skinned, childish and unable to take feedback. At the end of the meeting Marie leaves the room angered by Calvin's behaviour.

However, there was a quite different reality that Marie didn't see. In fact, Calvin had consciously decided before the meeting to do more listening instead of speaking and to be more enquiring – asking questions rather than giving his opinions. He has therefore been observing intently other team members at the meeting, but Marie has filtered out this information from her selection. It wasn't really something that she was looking for.

We can now see how Marie has constructed a set of beliefs about Calvin based on a series of selections and assumptions that have no basis in reality. Much of Marie's reasoning is illusion. Worse still, the next time Marie sees Calvin she is likely to use these preconceptions to inform her (mis)interpretation of new information, and so the loop continues (as shown in the arrow in the figure on page 125).

The whole process of going up the ladder of inference can happen in milliseconds. At each rung, there is a risk that values and assumptions held by the individual or team can skew the thinking process in a way that can lead to actions being taken that are either not based on reality or not likely to improve results or relationships.

Unless we become more aware, it is easy to get caught up in our own assumptions and delusions. By using the ladder of inference we can learn to slow down our thinking process and challenge our own and others' conclusions. Indeed, each of the four types of perception gap outlined in the first half of this chapter arise because individuals or teams have failed to challenge their own defective thinking. Either their selection from the available information is skewed or the way they interpret this information is flawed.

When using the ladder of inference to reduce inattentional blindness, there are some reflective questions we can ask at each rung on the ladder; in a group setting, it may be helpful to have the questions visible to help widen thinking.

Selection

- What information are we ignoring?

- What useful information have we filtered out?

- What are we not noticing that could be important?

- What other information could we draw upon?

- What have we missed?

Interpretation

- Are there other ways of interpreting the information we have?

- Can we look at this in a different way?

- What assumptions have we made?

- Are the assumptions we are using valid?

- How can we check our assumptions are correct?

- Are we allowing preconceptions to cloud our judgement here?

Conclusions

- Does this conclusion fit with what we have observed?

- What other conclusions could be drawn?

- Does the information we have lead us to only this conclusion?

Actions

- Will the actions we are planning to take address the issues we have identified?

- What other actions could be taken? What are the pros and cons of these alternatives?

Using the ladder of inference in this way provides an invaluable structured thinking process to evaluate whether unconscious bias is at work – bias that can lead to perception gaps.

Video analysis

Video analysis, applied in the right context, can be a hugely valuable approach if we want to eradicate inattentional blindness. Using video playback to analyse and reflect on the reality of an individual's or team's performance, rather than what is perceived to be happening, can be a powerful way to close perception gaps. Used effectively, the process can create much greater self-awareness of what works (and what doesn't) in a wide variety of contexts, including:

- Leading effective meetings

- Contributing to effective meetings

- Body language and performance skills

- Presenting and speech making

- Modelling and explaining

- Interacting with customers, clients and colleagues

- Coaching conversations

- Holding open-to-learning conversations

- Enquiry and sales dialogue

- Leading discussions

- Facilitating question-and-answer sessions

We have used video analysis as a core part of our training programmes over the last ten years. In education, for example, many teachers have had transformational personal epiphanies through analysing their performance on video. In many cases, they have been made powerfully aware of their unconscious competencies and incompetencies.[10] From our own research, one individual reflected that he had been in denial about a particular habit for many years. He had always dismissed feedback from colleagues about it – until one fateful day when he sat down to watch his video playback and was horrified by what he saw. He finally realised the truth of the common saying: 'You can't change what you're not aware of!'

---

10 See Adams, 'Learning a New Skill is Easier Said Than Done'.

Video playback offers individuals and teams the space and time to reflect on the quality and effectiveness of their performance. This provides two powerful outcomes. First, individuals frequently have 'eureka' moments when they discover aspects of their performance of which they were previously unaware. Those manifesting imposter syndrome are confronted by the enlightening reality that they are actually much better than they thought, while those burdened with the Dunning–Kruger effect cannot escape the fact that their performance is actually worse than they imagined.

It is impressive how much more open to learning these individuals become when they see evidence of their current performance level on video. Often, they are able to give themselves refreshingly honest feedback about their own performance that they would probably reject from colleagues or the team leader. Many reflect that viewing themselves from a third-person perspective makes it much easier to see how they can improve. Typical comments from individuals analysing their performance on video are: 'I realise now how many closed questions I ask'; 'My perception was that we spent an equal amount of time looking at the pros and cons – the reality was very different'; 'I really didn't check whether the team understood me properly'; 'I never realised I talked so much and listened so little'; and 'I didn't realise how my non-verbal communication contradicted the message I wanted to get across.'

The second outcome is just as powerful. Individuals begin to see the limitation of not noticing key information that is right in front of them. 'I need to work out how to be much, much better at noticing these things in real time' and 'I'm definitely going to listen with more of an open mind to feedback from others in future,' were two thoughtful reflections. This in-the-moment awareness is crucial if individuals are going to be effective at giving themselves more accurate and timely feedback.

Video analysis needs to be introduced sensitively if it is to increase openness to learning in teams. It is not uncommon to find expensive video technology still lying unused in the box in which it arrived, usually because one or more of the fundamentals outlined below has been overlooked.

Getting buy-in by agreeing protocols

Allay any possible nervousness or fear by setting out clear guidelines around confidentiality and the use and purpose of video analysis. Confidentiality agreements need the backing of a senior member of the organisation, and should state that the video can only be shared with others with the express permission of those being filmed. This is essential because if you want to use video analysis on an ongoing basis, you must have absolute trust and confidence from those involved that the purpose is developmental, rather than performance management by subterfuge. For some, the anticipation of being filmed is stressful enough, so it is important to create a safe, no-fail environment for them to learn more about their practice.

Make it clear that the sole purpose of the video analysis is as an aid to their learning and improvement. If necessary, where there are trust issues, make it an elective process. When the process is carried out with strong relational trust and clarity, you are likely to find that more people get involved as time goes on. If there is reluctance, be prepared as a team leader to embrace this new world and volunteer to go first.

Taking a micro focus

It is important to ensure that there is a clear focal point for the analysis. Without it, there is the risk that individuals are overwhelmed by the sheer amount of information to analyse in their video, which often prompts superficial feedback such as, 'I'm beginning to look and sound like my father!' It is unhelpful to reflect on too many aspects at once, so take a micro focus and make sure that those evaluating their performance pay attention to a few specific but key aspects of the agreed KASH of high performance.

Being clear on the focus for reflection plays a vital role in building trust in the process. One effective way to do this is to share in advance a list of reflective questions which individuals can focus on and answer while watching the playback. A valuable discussion to hold beforehand can be to ask participants, 'What would you like to be able to write in answer to these questions when you watch your video?' Positive visualisation can be a powerful strategy for improvement.

Building in planning and reflection time

We have found that it is essential to set aside time for the video feedback session as soon as possible after filming. Feedback and reflective dialogue three weeks after filming is likely to be of little use, as memories of the session will have faded. Unless time for the feedback session is ring-fenced in advance, the value and benefit of this work is likely to be diminished or even lost.

Making quality work publicly available

Case study: closing perception gaps

Simon was at the end of his tether. The team he'd led had received very negative feedback on their performance at a recent quality assurance visit. To Simon it was no surprise – the report was a fair and accurate assessment. But for a significant number of his team there was complete denial. Some individuals even wanted to appeal for a re-inspection. Before the assessment, Simon had tried in vain to engage staff in learning to develop their performance. However, he could see that his team were just paying lip service to the process. 'We don't need to change,' was a common refrain. As a result, performance had remained stubbornly stuck.

Five years later, the situation has radically changed. The team are now much more open to learning, and performance has improved. The catalyst for change was a visit Simon arranged for key influencers in his team to observe a similar team working in a much more challenging context. When the influencers returned, Simon was delighted. They had seen how much better the other team were at almost everything they did. In particular, they noted the culture of high expectations and team collaboration. They had been blown away by the experience. Now, with the scales removed from their eyes, they could see that their own team's performance was far from the level they had previously perceived. Simon had used the power of making best practice publicly available to help his team close their perception gaps.

When individuals and teams remain inward looking, high quality reference points on which to base self-perception can be lacking, leading to a risk of silo thinking. This is a common problem for those who don't regularly get to see the performance of their successful peers because they work alone or because the pace of work is too frenetic to process what is happening around them.

Reflection question

How often do your team members get to compare the quality of their work and outcomes with their peers or with similar teams elsewhere?

A fascinating characteristic of the most effective teams we have worked with has been the way they have taken the open sharing of good practice to a whole new level. For example, one team transformed their customer service provision following an idea that came directly from their leader's reflection on the fantastic service she had received in a restaurant. 'How do they do customer service so well?' was the question she had pondered about the wonderful experience. Her own team weren't in the catering industry themselves, but the principles of great customer service that the restaurant provided were eminently transferable. It is another example of looking for excellence.

Case study: making quality visible

Co-founder and head teacher Peter Hyman has a major focus on making quality visible at the pioneering School 21 which he leads in Stratford, London. Teaching staff build portfolios of learners' work to share with colleagues at specially organised events. This builds a shared understanding of quality. It also creates rich dialogue between staff about the teaching processes that led to its creation.

Feedback from others

The second essential element in minimising perception gaps is designing an environment in which feedback from others is highly effective. A client of ours, the leader of an organisation recognised nationally for its outstanding performance, reflected on the key role that effective feedback has played in their journey to excellence. 'Before we had effective feedback in place, too many people had overinflated perceptions of their performance. It was the first thing that hit me when I took over the organisation,' was his candid appraisal.

Consider these two questions:

1   To what extent is the feedback process in your own team designed to prevent perception gaps developing?

2   Is there shared clarity in your team about the feedback process?

Think for a moment about the verb 'design'. Designing is a process in which we envisage a finished product and then create a plan to get there. As we have already said, we are great believers in planning backwards from a beautiful outcome. It is the notion of reverse engineering.

What are sound principles for designing high quality feedback? Effective feedback should ensure that each individual understands how well they are performing and what they need to do to develop further. In our view, effective feedback should always be considered as a gift. It is something that is given and received to enhance one another's lives. Therefore, we should welcome receiving it in the same spirit in which we offer it to others. Even when feedback challenges us to change behaviour it is still a gift. We call it tough love.

What underpins effective feedback, including tough love, is that it is kind, specific and helpful.[11] Feedback designed using these principles has more chance of being listened to and acted upon.

---

11 These principles are inspired by Ron Berger's excellent book, *An Ethic of Excellence: Building a Culture of Craftsmanship with Students* (Portsmouth, NH: Heinemann, 2003).

Kind

The feedback process needs to be kind. As one leader put it, 'It's all about PIP [praise in public] and RIP [reprimand in private] for me.' In other words, he provides positive feedback in public and generally reserves any negative feedback for the privacy of his office, to avoid any feelings of public humiliation and the ill-feeling that may result. After all, the feedback process should honour the principles of relational trust that we examined in Chapter 4; in particular, professional and personal regard.

Case study: a lesson in damaging trust

The Etihad Stadium, 26 December 2008. The referee has blown the whistle for half-time. Hull City are already losing 4-0 to Manchester City. Hull's manager, Phil Brown, is furious. He decides to abandon the traditional half-time team talk in the warmth of the dressing room. Instead, he sits the team down on the pitch in front of an astonished crowd and gives them a very public dressing down. It created a huge talking point for the nation's media. Brown defended his decision, arguing that his team had let down their fans. As to whether it was effective or not, their results for the rest of the season provide an unequivocal answer – Hull won only one of their remaining nineteen league games!

We may never have been given humiliating feedback in front of millions watching on TV, yet many of us can probably relate to situations where a lack of personal or professional regard has meant that the feedback message has been overshadowed by the insensitivity with which it was delivered.

Where feedback is perceived to be unkind there are commonly two causes:

1   The feedback focuses on the person rather than on their behaviours or actions. This can lead to the receiver feeling as if they are being targeted

personally. The risk is that they will close down to protect their sense of self-worth and become less open to feedback in the future. Our suggestion is to always give feedback – positive or critical – on behaviour.

2   The feedback doesn't take into account any improvement in an individual's performance. By recognising and acknowledging this improvement, those receiving feedback feel that their effort and journey have been noticed and validated. In particular, those struggling with imposter syndrome feel encouraged to challenge their limiting assumptions and stretch their horizons. Our suggestion is to give immediate affirmation for any improvement in performance.

Reflection question

Does feedback in your team take into account personal and professional regard for others?

Specific

Providing specific feedback, especially about effective behaviours or areas to develop, helps others to realise exactly what they did well or need to change. If we want others to better articulate what they are doing well, then we need to help them understand and deconstruct this.

A good example of how not to do it occurred when we were working to evaluate the quality of feedback taking place within a team. We were reduced to open-mouthed incredulity when one individual mentioned that he'd received the following feedback from his team leader on how to improve his performance: 'There's a certain something missing.' If ever a piece of feedback was guaranteed to frustrate, mystify and confuse, this was it! Our suggestion is to be specific.

Being explicit about *what* was done well, and drawing out an understanding of good practice by asking *how* they did it, all helps. One of the best ways to reinforce good practice is with authentic, emotionally positive comments such as, 'I loved the way you went through the document with such care and generated those questions. Without them we wouldn't have got that contract.'

Where feedback is vague, it makes improvement more difficult and creates the perception among some individuals that becoming a high performer is nigh on impossible; whereas feedback that is specific effectively signposts the behaviours required. Ambiguous feedback can leave the receiver unclear about their level of performance and their strengths and weaknesses – perfect conditions for perception gaps to grow. On the other hand, specific feedback indicates clearly what behaviours are required to achieve great results.

A powerful technique for ensuring highly specific feedback is as follows:

1   Be explicit about the particular behaviour you are focusing the feedback on and the impact it had – for example, 'When you gave me strong eye contact in the presentation, it made me feel seen and connected with …'

2   Suggest how this feedback can develop performance further – for example, '… and what I suggest is that you share such eye contact with everyone in the meeting, not just with me and a couple of others.'

Reflection question

Is the feedback in your team specific? Does it ensure that all are crystal clear on their strengths and weaknesses?

Helpful

Feedback is helpful if the receiver is able to use it to be clearer on whatever good practice they already have, and gain clarity on whatever actions they need to take to improve their performance. Where we have observed or experienced helpful feedback, the receiver is left absolutely sure about what they need to do to improve and what steps are necessary to get there. It helps too when those giving feedback ask themselves, 'Does my feedback help the receiver to be clear about the next level of performance, and how to get there?'

Timing is a key ingredient in ensuring that feedback is helpful, both in terms of its proximity to the event and in ensuring that sufficient time is devoted to it. Proximity means that the experience is fresh and the mind is more likely to be open. Sufficient time means that the feedback can be properly absorbed and digested.

For example, we know of one team who work in a high pressure environment who make a point of holding a daily end-of-shift feedback session. They debrief the successes of the day as well as any events that have gone less well. The immediacy of the feedback ensures that the team learn to amend their behaviours quickly and can put changes in place the next day. Sometimes this dialogue is brief, but when problems have arisen the team are given enough time to ensure that everyone is clear about whatever lessons are to be learned and on the next steps to improve performance.

 Reflection question

Does feedback in your team provide helpful step change advice as well as signposting the desired performance?

Mastering open-to-learning conversations

Feedback that is kind, specific and helpful is not just of value for those with imposter syndrome; it also supports the eradication of perception gaps caused by the Dunning–Kruger effect. But there are other ways we can manage an effective dialogue with individuals who underestimate or overestimate their performance. One powerful strategy is to employ a conversational, open-to-learning approach. This technique is particularly helpful for leaders who tend to shy away from giving challenging feedback because they feel uncomfortable with conflict.

At the heart of the approach is the simple equation: $E + R = O$.[12] E stands for *event*. An event is any situation or relationship that needs to be explored or improved. R is our *reaction* to the event. O stands for the *outcome* that occurs as a result of the event and our reaction. This equation helps us appreciate the effect of our behaviour on others and on events. Our responses are always shaping the outcomes of events that happen around us, whether we are conscious of them or not. Taking no action is also a reaction, and therefore we have to take ownership for the impact of our reactions, or lack of them.

If our reaction to an event – for example, underperformance or being closed to learning – is to ignore it, then this is our choice, and there will be inevitable consequences that attend our choice. It may be that team members see this as an acceptance of underperformance or as a sign that being closed to learning is acceptable.

Another consequence might be that an individual's perception gap about their performance increases. 'After all,' they say to themselves, 'if there was a problem with my performance, then someone would surely have raised it with me.' Another effect might be that the leader's personal frustration with underperformance, or the lack of openness to learning in the team, remains.

On the other hand, if we do tackle events head-on, but don't offer feedback which is kind, specific and helpful, there may be other undesirable outcomes and consequences. Individuals may become conscious that their performance is not acceptable, but if the relational trust has been compromised then there may well be resistance. 'Did you see how that was handled?', they may say. 'Is this the new way in which our team is going to be humiliated?' When individuals and teams

---

12 See http://jackcanfield.com/blog/the-formula-that-puts-you-in-control-of-success/.

put their focus on preserving their sense of self-respect, behavioural change is unlikely to happen.

There is a third way, though – which is to accept the challenge of sharing the concern in order to demonstrate a passion for excellence, while still securing a positive outcome.

Three tools are available to avoid these pitfalls (as well as inattentional blindness): effective listening, carefully designed dialogue to develop shared clarity, and strategies to challenge false assumptions in our thinking. If we keep these three strategies in mind, the process of holding open-to-learning conversations is quite simple.

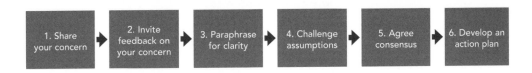

Step 1: Share your concern

Raise your concern and the reasons that have given rise to it. For example:

I've noticed that you've arrived late to work on five occasions in the last two weeks …

I'm not sure if I've got the whole picture, but I was worried when I saw/heard …

I have to share a concern I have regarding …

There may be more to this than I've seen so far, but when I read the latest sales report alarm bells began ringing in my head due to …

This approach can be challenging for leaders who find it difficult to have direct conversations. However, it is essential to clearly state the nature of the concern and the evidence you have for raising it. Key to the conversation is the sensitivity of the language used – for example, 'I noticed' rather than 'You did'. In this way, we are sticking to the principles underpinning the ladder of inference. All of us have our own view of the world and may not appreciate the big picture. Therefore, we share our concern, and the evidence we have for it, in order to explore the whole story, enquire into it and take corrective action if necessary.

Step 2: Invite feedback on your concern

The desired aim of this process is to resolve the issue and maintain relational trust with the colleague or team. This step provides your team member with the opportunity to offer their perspective about your concern.

Some useful language:

What's your take on what I've just said?

I realise that there may be more to this than what I've just outlined …

I really need to understand more from you about this situation …

At this point, the issue may resolve itself, if your colleague is ready to concede that the issue raised does actually need addressing. If this happens, you can move straight on to step 6. If not, continue to step 3.

Step 3: Paraphrase the receiver's feedback for clarity

An essential element of this stage is to paraphrase the feedback received in step 2. This ensures that no further perception gaps arise between what has been said and what has been heard by either person. This avoids the risk of either party falling into the trap of hearing what they want or expect to hear rather than what is being said.

Some useful language:

Just to clarify, these are the two important points you've made …

Am I right in summarising that your position is …?

Is what you're saying …?

Step 4: Challenge key assumptions that underpin unsatisfactory performance

This is the most difficult and sensitive step. Careful listening and paraphrasing provides the opportunity to challenge whatever assumptions or preconceptions are sustaining the team member's unsatisfactory performance. Some of these beliefs may be held unconsciously, so the reasoning behind them needs to be surfaced and made explicit. Examples might include, 'The customer who complained was not one of our key ones,' which suggests that the team member has a belief that only big customers need looking after, or 'That supplier was very blunt on the phone to me,' which sidesteps the reason for the bluntness (e.g. the team member should have ensured the invoice was paid six months ago!).

Some useful language:

What leads you to that conclusion?

How would we know if your assumption was wrong?

What other possible causes could there be?

Is this the only reason for this outcome?

What evidence is there that this is true?

What else are we missing here?

Step 5: Agree consensus on the need for change

The aim of challenging assumptions and preconceptions in the previous step was to reduce barriers to the point where, even though there may not be complete agreement on the events of the past, focus can now turn to the future. The overarching aim of step 5 is to draw together divergent views in order to move to a position where a mutual commitment to improve can be established.

Some useful language:

I can see that we can't agree on the causes of the problem, but we both want to do something about it.

It sounds like we are both keen to move on and prevent this from recurring.

We both agree that the current situation is not sustainable as it is.

Step 6: Develop an action plan

Many development strategies go wrong because they miss this important final step. It is essential to put in place a robust performance plan with a clear and specific time frame. Verbal agreements about next steps are insufficient as words alone are too prone to misinterpretation. If there isn't a specific, timetabled plan, you may end up having the same conversation in three weeks' time, as nothing may have changed.

Some useful language:

Let's draw up a clear timetabled plan to resolve this.

Right, so you're going to go away and deal with those outstanding issues by Monday lunchtime of next week.

Let's make time to meet each Friday at 9 a.m. for the rest of the month to go over these reports together to make sure we're back on track.

Modelling the REFRESH principles

One of the key ingredients for persuading more reluctant individuals to become open to feedback is the leader's willingness to model the REFRESH principles themselves. In fact, we have never worked with a team that has effective feedback strategies in place where the leader has exempted himself or herself from the process. By walking the talk, the leader becomes an important role model. This might be through demonstrating an unquenchable curiosity and enquiring mind or by an openness to feedback that helps the team to move forward. Here are some simple ideas to ensure that feedback is valued and acted on – from the leader to the most junior employee.

Nurturing a culture of divergent and enquiring thinking

'It's fine to disagree as long as we don't become disagreeable' was a line that stuck with us as we observed a team leader embark on a drive for more divergent thinking in his team. He didn't want a room full of nodding heads when he or anyone else proposed new ideas. He wanted all ideas to be challenged and stress-tested. He wanted to make sure that any new suggestions were actually going to make a positive impact if implemented live.

For this to work, the culture has to be safe – people need to know that critical feedback is welcome and valued. A culture that welcomes challenge, creativity and innovation is essential if you want everyone in the team to feel confident about speaking up. If there is any sense of resistance to 'dissent' from management, don't be surprised if many team members just keep their heads down.

PMI

One way to draw out diverse thinking is to use Edward de Bono's PMI thinking framework: pluses, minuses and interesting questions.[13] This framework is particularly useful when a team needs to consider two or more opposing viewpoints, such as when discussing contentious issues or during decision making. This simple activity is astonishingly useful because it challenges everyone to consider a dilemma from different perspectives. Many individuals find looking beyond their own immediate opinions and values both startling and eye-opening. Indeed, this easy-to-use process takes them way beyond simplistic analysis based on nothing more than unthinking prejudice or gut feeling. A tip for those unfamiliar with its use is to ensure that equal time is spent on each column in order to avoid unintentional bias.

For example, we worked with a team who had a successful range of face-to-face training products, who were pondering whether they should invest time in developing a new range of online training services. The team leader, Claire, was leaning towards the idea. She had seen it working phenomenally well in a local

---

13 PMI was first described by Edward de Bono in *De Bono's Thinking Course: Powerful Tools to Transform Your Thinking* (London: BBC Active, 2006 [1982]), although he also employs the tool in his later work.

firm operating in a different market. However, there were others in the team who were more sceptical. To slow her own thinking down, Claire gathered the team together to conduct a PMI exploration to draw out all the pluses, minuses and interesting questions.

Pluses	Minuses	Interesting questions
We already have a strong brand image in the market.	Team currently lacks sufficient ICT skills to customise the platform.	Apart from the early adopters, how large is demand going to be in the market?
Large LinkedIn, Twitter and customer database that could be used to create demand for online training services.	A mix of large and small competitors with a strong online presence already exists in the market.	Will the existing office broadband support the service?
Commercial web conferencing platforms are available to host online services.	Danger that the new online training will 'cannibalise' demand for existing face-to-face training.	Will demand for services operate outside office hours?
An online training presence will make us appear innovative and up-to-date in the eyes of customers.		Will new training be needed, given that it is not being delivered face to face?
In an era of tightening budgets, this could prove to be a more cost effective service for customers.		Will the content of online training differ from the existing face-to-face training?
		Do we have the capacity to move into the new market without compromising our existing product range?

Pluses	Minuses	Interesting questions
		What is the likely price, and therefore revenue, to be earned through these online services?
		Could online services act as a follow-up to complement the existing face-to-face training?

The PMI chart, which Claire and the team produced collaboratively, revealed that there were far too many unanswered questions, and therefore risk factors, that needed to be addressed for an immediate decision to be made. Claire resolved to get the team to gather these answers before any decisions, one way or the other, could be made.

Making listening a habit

Inviting others to give you feedback informally and welcoming 360-degree feedback opportunities are two ways to model your own openness to feedback. Making time to listen on a regular basis will provide many ideas to develop the team further, as well as building relational trust. Of course, not all of it will be useful. It will always be necessary to sift the wheat from the chaff; after all, feedback is not the truth, it is just one person's truth. However, the importance of demonstrating that you are listening deeply and are open to feedback can be as valuable as the benefit gained from the feedback received.

Showing how you are responding to feedback

Listening to feedback is important; however, being seen to act on it reinforces and multiplies the value and power. A team in one organisation we worked with has a wall display in the canteen. On the left-hand side it says, 'You said', and lists suggestions and feedback given by the team; in the middle it says, 'What we're doing', followed by a list of actions taken to address the feedback; and on the right-hand side, under 'The impact', are the effects these suggestions have had. The high visibility location reminds everyone in the organisation that continuous learning and improvement is shaped and enhanced by feedback that is listened to and acted upon.

Reflection questions

Is making time for listening to others a well-developed habit for you?

Do you provide opportunities for all within your team to offer feedback?

Team language and the importance of words

Leaders who consistently use the language of 'we' and 'us' help to diminish individualism and promote a collaborative culture within the team. The great Brazilian footballer Pelé once said, 'no individual can win a game by himself'.[14] A collaborative culture discourages individuals with a high sense of self-worth from taking too much personal credit for team achievement and encourages those who lack confidence to take more credit for the contributions they make.

---

14 See Frank Malley, 'Pele, the Perfect Player', *The Independent* (23 December 1999). Available at: https://www.independent.co.uk/sport/football/international/pele-the-perfect-player-743002.html.

Another way to reinforce the importance and values of a team culture is to use quotes and affirmations, such as the examples below. You can pin them up on staff noticeboards or attach them to the bottom of emails to reinforce the notion that the team is bigger and more effective than any of its component individuals.

The ratio of We's to I's is the best indicator of the development of a team. – Lewis B. Ergen

Alone we can do so little. Together we can do so much. – Helen Keller

Many of us are more capable than some of us, but none of us is as capable as all of us. – Anon

Sticks in a bundle are unbreakable. – Kenyan proverb

Knowing your position on the learning–performance matrix lies at the heart of accurate self-perception. It is an essential foundation in ensuring that openness to learning is not inhibited by either overrating or underrating your own performance. Indeed, we've not worked with a high performing open-to-learning team where perception gaps are present or have been allowed to develop.

Maintaining accurate self-perception action plan
What could be the start/stop actions in terms of modelling REFRESH principles with others in your team? What could be the start/stop actions in terms of ensuring accurate self-feedback in your team? What could be the start/stop actions in terms of ensuring accurate feedback from others in your team?
Start actions
Stop actions

REFRESH reading list

Some suggested reading if you want to delve deeper:

Fisher, Roger and Ury, William (2012). *Getting to Yes: Negotiating an Agreement Without Giving in* (New York: Random House Business).

Kahneman, Daniel (2011). *Thinking, Fast and Slow* (London: Penguin).

Patterson, Kerry, Grenny, Joseph, Maxfield, David, McMillan, Ron and Switzler, Al (2013). *Crucial Accountability: Tools for Resolving Violated Expectations, Broken Commitments, and Bad Behavior*, 2nd edn (Columbus, OH: McGraw Hill Education).

Rosenberg, Marshall B. (2015). *Nonviolent Communication: A Language for Life* (Encinitas, CA: Puddle Dancer Press).

Stone, Douglas and Heen, Sheila (2015). *Thanks for the Feedback: The Science and Art of Receiving Feedback Well* (New York: Portfolio Penguin).

Part III
Designing effective learning

In Part I, we advocated the imperative for learning and highlighted the consequences of not nurturing a learning culture. We also introduced the learning–performance matrix which enables a team's starting points to be established, and we defined the learning destination – a team of high performers fully open to learning.

In Part II, we examined the main ingredients required to create an optimal team learning culture: building processing capacity, developing relational trust and ensuring accurate self-perception. We examined strategies to build up each element. However, by themselves these three important ingredients do not guarantee that effective learning and development will take place.

The purpose of this final part, therefore, is to help you design effective learning – learning that will make it possible for individuals and teams to move towards the open-to-learning/high performer quadrant of the matrix. Using a tried and tested planning process, which we call 'planning backwards',[1] the chapters in this part provide a step-by-step guide to designing high quality learning.

This process can be used to design effective learning regardless of whether it is a one-hour training event or a longer-term programme lasting several months. Given that your team might have a wide range of possible learning needs, we will use 'learning programme' as a generic term to cover all the different types of formal learning development that might be common in your field, such as conferences, workshops, e-learning, coaching and iterative training programmes. We will also use the term 'learner' to refer to those taking part in the learning programme. After all, that is what we are hoping they will be.

We will describe those putting together a plan for the learning programme as 'designers'. The word conveys the level of skill required to develop a learning programme that will meet the learning needs of the learners successfully. Just as a made-to-measure suit meets the needs of its wearer, so effective and memorable learning needs to aim at a perfect fit and therefore requires careful design. We will also describe how the proposed strategies and tools will ensure that cognitive capacity, strong relational trust and accurate self-perception are reinforced.

A planning template to assist you in designing learning programmes, based on this part of the book, is available in Appendix 2 and to download at: www.learningimperative.co.uk/downloads/planning-template.

---

1   Grant Wiggins and Jay McTighe, *Understanding by Design* (Alexandria, VA: Association for Supervision and Curriculum Development, 2005).

Chapter 6

Planning backwards

Cathy left the training session completely frustrated. Her day had started with a real sense of anticipation because she had heard so much about the new learning programme. However, it turned out to be an utter disappointment – she had spent the whole day listening to things she already knew. Given there was so much to do back in the office, another session like this could easily challenge her openness to the value of training.

- Have you ever been on a programme where you have learned nothing or very little?

- Are you keen to understand the principles of design which develop both learning and performance?

- Do you want to design learning programmes that inspire your team to move towards the open-to-learning/high performer quadrant of the learning–performance matrix?

What's in this chapter for me?

For the last ten years, we have been designing learning programmes for adults: some have been short sessions that have taken just a morning, while others have been extensive programmes that have lasted for a year. Many of these programmes have been run by ourselves or delivered by our team of trainers. We have also worked with in-house trainers in organisations to improve the quality of their own learning programmes. At the heart of every programme we design is the principle of planning backwards – a deceptively simple yet incredibly powerful tool for building effective learning.

In this chapter, we will explain the process of planning backwards and provide a step-by-step guide to how it can be used to design learning programmes. This process will prevent many of the elementary pitfalls, such as those which underpinned Cathy's bad experience, by ensuring that the learning programme design is specifically tailored to the needs of your team and their starting points.

What do we mean by planning backwards?

A. Current situation · B. Goal

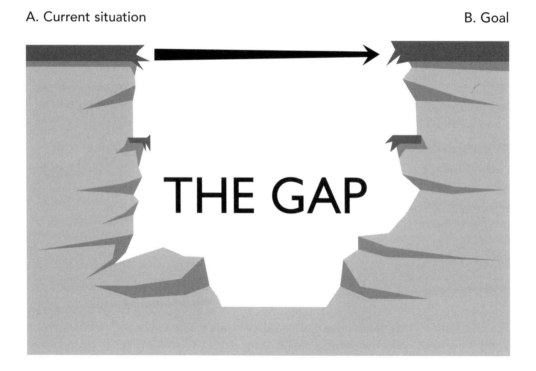

Planning backwards is a process that starts with the learning goal very clearly in mind. This learning process can be represented quite simply as a gap – a gap between the desired destination (KASH) and the starting position of the learners. For anyone designing a learning programme and hoping to ensure high impact, the challenge is to narrow this disparity.

Planning backwards involves a series of important steps even before the structure and content of the learning programme can be developed. These steps require the designer to first establish the desired outcome of the learning programme. We will explore this in more depth later in the chapter, but essentially it requires the designer to answer the following question: what are the precise aspects of knowledge, attitudes, skills and habits that this learning programme is seeking to build?

Once the learning destination has been determined, the next step is to establish the starting KASH of the learners who are taking part in the programme. What aspects of KASH do they have already?

Step 1
Define the KASH destination that the learning programme is seeking to achieve.

Step 2
Establish the KASH starting points of learners.

Step 3
Design a learning programme based on the identified gap.

The information gathered in steps 1 and 2 will help the designer to shape the structure, processes and content of the learning programme in order to close the gap. While planning backwards might seem obvious, we have witnessed too many ineffective learning programmes that have been compromised by a failure to clearly identify key information at steps 1 and 2. Cathy's dismal experience occurred because, for her, no gap at all had been designed into the programme.

In this chapter we will examine steps 1 and 2 in depth, while step 3 will be the focus of Chapters 7 and 8. Chapter 7 will explain how to make sure there is shared clarity about the KASH destination and how to get there. Chapter 8 will detail how to ensure that there are high quality opportunities to practise and master the new KASH.

Step 1: Define the KASH destination

The first stage requires the designer to establish clearly the ideal outcome of the programme. What precisely is this learning programme hoping to achieve? What would 'perfect' or 'excellent' look, sound and feel like in terms of the KASH development of those taking part? Two key principles underpin the art of planning backwards. The first is clarity, which we will explore below. The second is to strenuously avoid any temptation to make assumptions by establishing learners' actual starting points, which we will cover in step 2.

Why is it so critical to clearly define the learning destination?

Unless learning objectives are carefully and specifically defined, the openness to learning of those taking part and the effectiveness of the learning programme are at risk. As we highlighted in Chapter 2, poorly designed learning doesn't just have zero impact, it often has an adverse impact.

Where the learning destination is fuzzy and ill-defined, there is a much greater likelihood of cognitive overload. If the designer is unclear about the precise learning destination, it is very likely that learners will become confused and frustrated. Furthermore, in our experience, lack of clarity in programme design often leads to the insertion of far too much content. As we explained in Chapter 3, too much information, particularly when it is not specifically targeted, contributes to the risk of cognitive overload among learners.

Case study: death by PowerPoint

A sales team who had endured a diet of unfocused learning programmes made their own fun to keep themselves 'engaged'. They invented a game which they played whenever they were on the receiving end of a PowerPoint-heavy training session. They called it PowerPoint Lotto. Before entering the training room, they each made a prediction about the number of slides that would be shown in the session. The person whose prediction was furthest away from the actual number would have to buy coffees for the rest of the team!

Where the learning destination is sharply focused, feedback immediately becomes more effective. If, for example, there are three specific aspects of KASH that need improvement, this will automatically provide a precise focus for the programme leader to target specific feedback on learner progress, or its absence. Time for practice and feedback is key, so if there is not enough time to cover everything then our strong advice is to include fewer topics.

One of the most important motivators for learners is the feeling of developing competency that comes with successful learning. This particularly applies when a learner's profile is towards the closed-to-learning end of the continuum. Designers need to build in early opportunities for learners to experience their competence growing. Nothing creates a positive mindset as powerfully as the experience of success, especially for those who have, over the years, created a negative internal dialogue about failure and self-doubt. When achievable activities and clearly defined KASH outcomes are designed into the programme, there is much more chance that learners will recognise their developing proficiency.

Where the learning destination is clearly stated, there is much less likelihood of valuable time being wasted on unnecessary content or processes. At every stage of the process, designers should ask themselves the following question: does each element, step by step, help to build the KASH we want learners to have acquired by the end of the programme? If so, keep it. If not, bin it! Planning backwards from a specific learning destination avoids irrelevant content being included and maximises time for developing the desired KASH.

Case study: learning programme to develop teacher quality

We were invited to work with the learning programme designers for a large school network. They were reflecting on the low impact of some of their programmes on improving teacher performance, in spite of positive evaluations given by attending delegates. Part-way through this conversation one of the designers had a 'eureka' moment: 'We want to help teachers develop their questioning skills, but we are not giving them any opportunities to practise these skills "live" in their classrooms or receive in-the-moment focused feedback.' The important connection between the learning destination and the programme was made. And with it, a step change improvement in how the designers would plan in the future.

Absolute clarity about the KASH destination enables the designer to shape the ideal structure and sequence of the learning programme. If the learning programme specifically aims to build learners' skills, for example, then the structure of the programme must provide opportunities for them to practise those skills and gain feedback on their skills development.

By planning the programme backwards from the desired outcome, designers can identify the most logical sequence so that learners are presented with new learning in the most coherent and user-friendly way. Designers can ask themselves: what is the first stage in the learning process, and what will then follow? In the following case study, careful identification of the KASH required really helped to sharpen the sequencing of learning.

Case study: reorganising learning

Some time ago, we were invited to support a large retail organisation to redevelop a learning programme for their new staff. The first thing we did was to analyse their existing offering. This programme was presented as a series of sessions, each focusing on how to sell a particular product line: shoes, homeware, womenswear and so on. It struck us that there was substantial repetition within the sessions. Each session treated the sales process for each product line as unique. When we analysed the sessions, it became clear that while there were small differences between selling furniture and shoes, around 90% of the sales process was identical, irrespective of the product. The programme, as it stood, made the learning process overly complicated for new staff.

We suggested that they redesign the programme to make the similarities of each product line much clearer to new staff. Thus, instead of learning nine different sales processes, they in fact needed only one, with bespoke aspects for each different product line. As a result, the learning programme was restructured so that new staff were trained first on the generic sales process, and then received shorter sessions on each of the bespoke parts of the different product lines. This approach reduced cognitive overload and helped new staff to see the similarities and differences between the selling of each product. It also ensured that time off the shop floor in training was reduced, giving staff more time to practise their skills with real customers.

Designer action points

Use the planning template in Appendix 2 to address the following challenges about any learning programmes you are currently designing:

What is the specific knowledge you want learners to acquire by the end of the programme?

What attitudes do you want learners to develop by the end of the programme (e.g. enthusiasm and commitment to implementing change within their job role)?

What skills do you want learners to develop by the end of the programme?

What are the specific habits you want learners to embed by the end of the programme?

Careful reflection on these questions will pay great dividends in the long term. It will make planning much easier and you will avoid the pitfalls of creating insufficiently thought-out training programmes. The key is to make sure that your answers to the above questions are really specific. Check, before starting, that you have accurate information on the specific KASH development that is desired.

Here is an example of a set of tightly defined KASH objectives for a learning programme we recently designed:

Learners will:

- Understand the main reasons for some delegates on their programmes being closed to learning.

- Develop the knowledge and skills to build personal and professional regard with delegates.

Step 2: Establish the KASH starting points of learners

Not making assumptions about what learners do and don't already know is the second key principle to keep in mind when planning backwards. Cathy's poor experience, described at the start of this chapter, was mainly caused by the course designer's supposition that the content would be new for all delegates.

It is equally important not to make overestimations of learners' starting points. When this is the case, learners will lack the basic knowledge and understanding on which the new programme is built. They will feel out of their depth and unable to connect because the new learning is too cognitively complex for them to grasp. This can easily reinforce any negative beliefs they may hold that learning is just too hard.

Our advice to anyone, but especially learning designers, is to beware of assumptions. This becomes immediately obvious when we recognise that making assumptions is synonymous with guessing. If you hear yourself, or anyone else, saying things like, 'They should know X already', 'They should remember this from last year' or 'I don't think they will have come across this before', then alarm bells should start ringing.

No learning designer worth their salt would deliberately set out to design a programme based on guesswork, but we have come across plenty who have made the mistake of basing their design on postulations – with all the negative consequences for learning. Instead, ask yourself: what feedback have I used to inform whatever assumptions I'm holding, and how accurate are they? This is not very different from the approach we took when examining the ladder of inference back in Chapter 5.

Accurate pre-assessment has numerous benefits when it comes to designing an effective learning programme, as it:

Enables the impact of the learning programme to be measured

When learners' starting points are established, rather than assumed, it is much easier to measure the programme's impact on the development of their KASH. When pre-assessment is not carried out, there is always a risk that the success of a programme will be overestimated. This happens, for example, when learners start a programme already having some of the KASH that it seeks to develop. In these circumstances, post-course evaluation will overrate the effectiveness of the programme.

Enables effective tailoring of learning programme design

Effective pre-assessment helps to flag up the different starting points of the learners taking part. This enables designers to consider how they will adjust the structure and content of the programme to meet learners' differing needs. It avoids the dreaded 'sheep dip' approach where everyone gets the same treatment! For example, in the case of the retailer redesigning their new starter programme, pre-assessment identified which new staff had previous retail experience and in which product lines. This enabled the designers to develop a learning programme that fast-tracked these individuals through those elements of the programme in which they already had the desired KASH.

In other cases, pre-assessment will indicate that designers need to start at step 1 of the planning backwards process – for example, when it turns out that, given the learners' starting points, the learning destination is too challenging without additional support. On the other hand, it may be the case that the envisaged learning destination won't provide any improvement because learners already possess the KASH that the programme aims to develop.

Aids the collation of misconceptions and possible areas of confusion

Pre-assessment provides the opportunity to discover any misconceptions or areas of confusion that learners may hold about the planned programme's content. This is essential information for the programme designer. Where confusion and misconceptions are identified, the programme can be adapted to spend more time on addressing them. Without this feedback, there is the risk that these misconceptions may remain and hinder learners' progress.

Establishes the level of openness to learning

A crucial role of pre-assessment is to establish not just the knowledge, skills and habits of the learners, but also their attitudes towards learning. Again, this is essential information for the learning programme designer. We observed an example of this recently where an organisation was seeking to improve the performance of its key staff. It had looked at implementing a learner-led programme that had worked particularly well in a similar organisation locally. However, when they analysed the attitude of their staff, they realised there were far fewer self-starters in their organisation. Left to lead their own learning, few would have been likely to have done so successfully; therefore, they adapted the programme's design so that it was more directive.

Builds confidence

A final benefit of pre-assessment is building learner confidence in the programme itself. When designers, in advance of the programme, ask, 'What can you do already?' and 'What would you like to be able to do as a result of the programme?', participants can feel directly involved in both the design and the relevance of the programme. We remember chatting to a group of staff who were hugely positive about the value of a programme in which they had recently taken part. One of the aspects they really appreciated was that the learning was needs led: 'They always listen to, and take into account, the feedback we give them about what we need more learning time on. It makes us feel our voice is valued.'

Strategies and tools for establishing starting points

If a learning programme is going to be based on feedback, rather than assumptions and guesswork, how can pre-assessment be done quickly and effectively? In this section, we will provide some straightforward and proven ways to gather this information.

Pre-programme questionnaire

A pre-programme questionnaire is a really valuable way to engage all participants in pre-assessment. One approach is an online survey which seeks to establish what delegates see as their own starting points, and what they would like to achieve from the programme. For an example of a pre-course questionnaire, please visit: www.learningimperative.co.uk/downloads/pre-assessment.

The exact content of the questionnaire will vary depending on what the programme hopes to develop. However, it could focus on one or more of the following aspects:

■ Discovering whether the assumed starting points for knowledge, attitudes and skills are accurate.

- Seeking feedback on areas in which learners feel they lack confidence or competence.

- Identifying aspects of the programme that learners need more/less focus on.

- Discovering learners' previous training experience in this area.

- Finding out about aspects of their job role/experience if this information is not readily available.

- Enquiring into their hopes and fears about the programme.

In some cases, for example with smaller groups, this pre-assessment can be a face-to-face meeting. This has the added advantage of creating an opportunity to develop relational trust with, and between, the group.

On-the-day needs analysis

If pre-assessment can't take place before the start of the programme, the next best solution is to carry out a full needs analysis with the learners at the start of the session. This enables the programme leader to skilfully adapt the session to better meet the needs of those taking part. It can also have the effect of helping to get buy-in from those learners who may be questioning the value of the programme.

Some useful question prompts to establish starting points include:

- What specifically do you want to do differently as a result of this programme?

- What are the key parts of your role that you would like to develop through this programme?

- What other training have you had already in this area?

- What is your role, and how long have you been in it?

- What do you see as your strengths in this area, and what are possible areas for development?

Where are learners on the learning–performance matrix?

The position of individuals on the learning–performance matrix (see Chapter 2) will provide an important source of feedback to aid pre-assessment, especially when designing learning programmes for learners with whom you are not familiar.

As a designer, there are some useful questions to ask team leaders in order to deepen your understanding of the feedback received from the pre-assessment:

■ Where would you place each individual in your team on the matrix? Why have you placed them there?

■ What qualitative/quantitative feedback underpins your judgement?

■ Have any team members shifted their position on the matrix over the last two years? If so, what were the causes?

■ What are the key aspects of each team member's KASH that is preventing them from raising their performance?

■ If individuals are positioned near the closed-to-learning end of the continuum, what are the causes?

Using the matrix to identify the causes of underperformance or being closed to learning (rather than the effects) really helps organisations and team leaders to define exactly what they want from a learning programme.

Adapting learning based on pre-assessment

When learners make the effort to respond through pre-assessment, it is crucially important that designers use and incorporate this feedback. This sends out a powerful message to learners that their feedback has played a role in shaping the design of the programme so that it meets their specific needs. It is useful to include these changes in the introduction to the programme – both as evidence that the designer has listened, and to demonstrate why the objectives of the programme are as they are.

All feedback from the pre-assessment process should help to answer the key questions that are essential for the design of a successful learning programme:

■ How big is the gap between the starting points and the desired destination?

■ Do we have the time, and other relevant resources, to successfully close this gap?

■ What are the specific changes in KASH that will occur if the learning programme successfully closes the gap?

A word of caution regarding feedback: any feedback gathered during the pre-assessment, no matter how thorough, may not actually represent the whole picture. Pre-assessment provides valuable insights into the starting points of learners, but only to the extent of their own awareness and experience. It is the role of the designer and trainer to stretch and expand these parameters in the design and then the delivery of the course.

To illustrate what we mean, the late, great John Peel, BBC Radio 1's late night show DJ for over thirty years, is a great example. His passion for championing new music was legendary. He had a unique approach: he didn't only give listeners what they wanted, he also gave them music they didn't know they would enjoy. In other words, until people heard the music, they couldn't develop a desire for listening to or buying it. The same principle applies to learning and programme design too. The organisation, the individuals and the teams may think they know what they want, but the skill of the programme designer and the trainer is to provide both this and the elements they don't yet know about to optimise the learning experience for everyone taking part.

Getting buy-in from learners from the outset

If a learning programme is to be effective, a fundamental starting point is that the learners need to be open to learning. Where pre-assessment indicates that learners are not, designers and course leaders have two stark choices: try to do something about it or do nothing and suffer the consequences. In this section we will set out some proven strategies to get buy-in from those taking part.

Shaping the learning environment

It is amazing how paying careful attention to the learning environment can play a positive role in shaping a group's openness to learning. First of all, ensure that learners' basic needs (food, drink, ambient temperature, natural light, suitable background music, comfortable seating) have been met. This demonstrates a subtle but genuine personal regard for those taking part. Second, offer a warm welcome and make introductions if learners have not met or worked together before. It is always useful to get learners speaking early on. This encourages their participation, as they hear their own voice in the group and are encouraged to speak up more. These are small but significant signs that those attending are part of a valued learning community.

Now ask yourself:

- Will the room and layout be conducive to learning?

- Is it a welcoming environment?

- How can I nurture a sense of safety and inclusion in the learning environment?

- How can I create an authentic learning environment that is related to, but not disturbed by, the busy world of work?

Meeting the needs of learners

In Chapter 4, we explained how demonstrating personal regard is essential in building relational trust based on learners' personality traits. These personality traits also have an impact on how and why they react to learning in different ways.

Some will buy in to a programme because of its relevance to their needs, so make the programme's relevance crystal clear. Conducting a needs analysis and careful pre-assessment will be really important in ensuring their learning needs are met.

Others may be influenced by the human connection – working closely with their programme leader and colleagues. For these individuals, a warm welcome and activities to build relationships, especially where learners are not from the same team or organisation, is crucial.

For other learners, their connection with the programme will be an opportunity for deep thinking, reflection and personal growth. They may well want information about any research underpinning the key messages, as well as sufficient reflection time to consider and analyse issues.

Finally, there may be learners who will buy into a programme because of the opportunities for interaction, innovation and creativity.

Designers and programme leaders therefore need to consider and integrate the diversity of personality traits and learning preferences when considering how to secure buy-in to a programme.

Establishing clear protocols

An essential tool in helping everyone to feel comfortable, which in turn builds stronger relational trust, is the use of a programme protocol. The protocol sets out the ways in which everyone will interact during the programme. This ensures confidentiality and supports a sense of safety, so people will speak openly and make themselves vulnerable by asking questions such as, 'Can you explain that again? I don't understand.'

An organisation we worked with some years ago struggled to ensure that its employees were open to learning on their development programmes for store managers. The managers had training sessions together several times a year to explore ways to improve performance in the stores they led. However, because they perceived that any problems they shared would be fed back to senior leaders, not one of them ever admitted to having a single problem in their own store, particularly when that problem could be attributed to themselves! As a result, the training had no significant impact on their development.

The solution was to draw up a confidentiality protocol that everyone signed on arrival. It could be summarised as follows: what we disclose in this room is shared to enrich our learning and development as managers. It will not be used as part of any management performance evaluation.

The next training session was a revelation. The managers spoke openly about their problems, many of which were caused by central systems and processes. They were so energised by the discussion around one particular process glitch that they came up with a series of improvement recommendations that they all agreed needed to be fed back to the support team. As one manager commented, 'I used to come along under sufferance, bemoaning a day out of store. Now I genuinely look forward to the rich learning that comes from these days.'

The programme protocol can play a key role in building trust between the programme leader and the delegates. It can detail the rights and responsibilities of both parties, and establish a safe environment for everyone to discuss issues related to the learning programme. We suggest it should also encourage the adoption of unconditional positive regard when delegates are talking about others who are not present.

Modelling the importance of listening and acting on feedback

As we stressed in Chapter 4, listening to feedback, and being seen to act on it, is essential in building trust. Individuals can become closed to learning simply because they don't feel heard or appreciated by the programme leader. Here are some ways to ensure people feel valued:

- Conduct a public needs analysis at the programme's outset. This is a great way to demonstrate that the participants' views are important. Revisit them from time to time to discuss and demonstrate how these needs are being met.

- When learners make interventions that could potentially take a session off course, or if issues are raised that will be dealt with at a later stage, add them to a snag list on a flip chart. This publicly demonstrates that these points are important and will be addressed at a more convenient time.

- Listen carefully, paraphrasing key points made by learners. In this way everyone in the room is clear on the conversation. Model the principles of unconditional regard. This includes showing gratitude for learners who demonstrate personal vulnerability through the contributions they make.

- Seek regular feedback from learners on the value of the programme so that any queries or concerns can be addressed immediately.

Framing the dialogue

On occasion, learning programmes can be undermined by negativity and an over-focus on problems and blame rather than learning and ownership. Where closed mindsets exist, blaming others about the failings of the past can prevail, and learning and change become difficult to achieve.[1] Using a tool such as 'locus of control' can really help to frame the learning dialogue. The following example shows how a trainer redefined the thinking of two individuals who had a well-developed negative mindset.

Dave and Ian were classics of their type. Some of their colleagues called them Statler and Waldorf after the two old hecklers on the balcony in *The Muppet Show*. Whenever they were on a course they would try to steer conversations towards the ills of the organisation, their own workload and the failings of various

---

1   J. B. Rotter, 'Generalized Expectancies for Internal Versus External Control of Reinforcement', *Psychological Monographs: General & Applied*, 80(1) (1966), 1–28.

managers. For everyone else in the room, it made the sessions seem like wading through mud.

One day, however, they met their match. An external course leader had been invited in to work with Dave, Ian and their colleagues. The leader had done a full pre-assessment and was ready with a plan to switch the dialogue from one dominated by problems and blame to one about ownership and possibilities. She simply drew two concentric circles on the flip chart like this:[2]

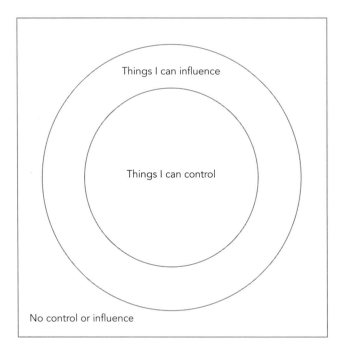

The circles represent three areas. The inner circle represents what the individual or team can control, the outer circle what they can influence and the area outside the concentric circles what they can't control or influence.

Each time Dave and Ian fell into their timeworn narrative, the course leader challenged them to consider where the problem would be classified on the locus of

---

2   See http://www.talkingabout.com.au/3ControlInfluenceConcern.

control. Were these problems they could address by taking action themselves, or were these problems they could influence? The conversations that took place helped them both to understand that they could take a great deal more owner- ship than they had hitherto realised. It also helped them see that it was much more rewarding to focus on solutions than problems.

And, of course, if there were problems that they couldn't control or influence, then the leader posed the question: 'If there is nothing you can do to control or influence this issue, might it be better to just let it go?' Sometimes, we just have to recognise the limitations of our control and influence.

Modelling the attitudes you are seeking to nurture

Perhaps the most persuasive skill for achieving buy-in from learners is for the programme leader to model the attitudes he or she is hoping to nurture in oth- ers. We suggest that you revisit the REFRESH learning model and ask yourself the following questions:

■ How can I, as a course leader, model *resilience* in learning?

■ How can I demonstrate that I have a curious and *enquiring* approach?

■ In what ways can I show that I value and act on *feedback*?

■ Am I constantly seeking ways to *revise* the programme, and how I lead it, to improve its impact on the learning of others?

■ How can I demonstrate that *effort* and openness are key to learning and personal growth?

■ Where are there opportunities to showcase the power of *sharing* and collaboration?

■ How can I model that learning is most valuable when it is *habitual*?

All the impactful learning programmes we've come across have one thing in com- mon: they have been planned backwards. It's a process that will help you to maximise the impact of learning for your team. By having absolute clarity, not only on the KASH you are seeking to develop in learners, but also their starting points, you'll be able to ensure that they have a manageable gap to close on the programmes you lead.

REFRESH reading list

Some suggested reading if you want to delve deeper:

Brown, Peter C., Roediger, Henry L. and McDaniel, Mark A. (2014). *Make It Stick: The Science of Successful Learning* (Cambridge, MA: Harvard University Press).

Hattie, John and Yates, Gregory C. R. (2014). *Visible Learning and the Science of How We Learn* (Abingdon: Routledge).

Chapter 7

Developing shared clarity

Michael was shaking his head in amazement. He was a team leader lost in a maze, trying to bring about improvement in his team. Nothing he tried had worked. At a loss, he brought in an external learning programme provider. He was shaking his head because this programme seemed to cover exactly the same material that he had covered, yet it was having a radically different impact on his team. 'It's been transformative,' he observed. 'I watched the training sessions and staff began to develop a shared language about excellence. It's even influencing conversations in the office among individuals who I thought were completely closed to learning.' The new programme was more effective because of the clarity of its key messages. Michael's revelation was echoed in the girl band Bananarama's hit of the 1980s: 'It ain't what you do, it's the way that you do it, and that's what gets results.'

Michael's experience demonstrates the importance of developing shared clarity if we want to overcome barriers to learning. As we explored in Part II, shared clarity provides two powerful buy-ins. First, it reduces cognitive overload by giving learners clarity about their learning gaps and how to close them. Instead of feeling overwhelmed, shared clarity diminishes the uncertainty that learning new knowledge, attitudes, skills and habits can bring. Second, it accelerates relational trust between learners and trainers. When programme leaders model and explain new learning, and the reasons for it, clearly and concisely, they are actively demonstrating their competence.

■ Have you ever been on a learning programme and felt overwhelmed by new information?

- Are you keen to understand how to hook others into learning by making it clearer and more doable?
- Are you seeking practical tools and strategies to develop shared clarity with those you lead?

What's in this chapter for me?

In this chapter, we will first revisit what we mean by shared clarity and the ingredients that underpin it. Then we will describe a simple and effective three-stage model to build shared clarity with learners. This model combines the two principles of planning backwards: the importance of clarity and the danger of making assumptions. We will also provide proven tools and strategies to ensure that learners on your programmes reap the full benefits of shared clarity. These tools and strategies will help with clarity across the programme and also within individual sessions.

What do we mean by shared clarity?

Shared clarity happens when leader and learners have a common understanding of the answers to three fundamental questions: why, what and how? Depending on the learner, and their starting point as plotted on the learning–performance matrix, they may have formulated answers to these questions already. However, we need to ensure that their answers are the same as ours. The beauty of these three questions is that they can be applied to the programme as a whole as well as to each individual session within it.

Why?

'Why' is the first and most powerful of the three questions. It is the question that may underlie one or more of the following variants that are asked or pondered by delegates on learning programmes:

- Why do I need this?

- Why should I commit time to or prioritise this?

- Why do I need to improve my performance?

- Why would I benefit from this?

- Why do I need this on top of my existing workload?

The answers to these questions provide learners with the hook and motivation to engage in the learning programme. They also provide justification for the programme that we can refer to when, for example, learners challenge the need for, or rationale of, the programme. A powerful re-statement and justification of the 'why' can have a profoundly positive impact on those who are closed to learning.

What?

'What' provides learners with clarity about the process and what the end result will look like. It also provides key information and knowledge that learners will need to help them move their learning forward, such as overcoming possible difficulties and challenges that may arise. The 'what' question will help learners to answer the following:

- What is the big picture?

- What is the difference between what I currently do and this new approach?

- What are the connections between what I am learning about today and the big picture?

- What is the reasoning or research behind this change?

- What are the tricky parts of this new learning?

- What are the potential problems I need to be aware of?

- What feedback will tell me that I am on the right track?

- What are the thinking steps or stages in the process that have to be followed?

- What are the key principles that I need to grasp?

How?

Learners may feel frustrated if the 'how' question is left unanswered. Unless they have tools, strategies and step-by-step support to get from their individual starting points to their desired destination, they are likely to get stuck.

Shared clarity about the 'how' will enable you to address fundamental questions that may well be in learners' minds:

- How will they be able to apply what they are learning and get feedback?

- What are the tools or strategies that they will be able to use, and how do they use them?

- How will they get started?

- How can they overcome problems that might arise?

- How will it help them to improve their performance?

- Where might they get further help and guidance?

- How will they know they are making good progress or need support?

- What are the stages in the process that will help them to improve their performance?

Of course, there may be individuals on a programme who already have answers to the what and why questions, but these tend to be the people in the open-to-learning/high performer quadrant of the learning–performance matrix. Ensuring shared clarity on the what, why and how provides the maximum chance for all learners to develop and improve their performance on the programme.

Designer action points

In order to achieve shared clarity, what would be the specific answers to the three questions below for a learning programme you are currently working on?

Why?

What?

How?

Me, we, you

In this section, we will examine ways to ensure that there is shared clarity around why, what and how. To achieve this, we will use the *me, we, you model*. The three-stage model is a deceptively simple yet highly effective way of ensuring shared clarity between programme leaders and learners at any point on a learning programme.

The model starts with the *me* stage, during which the programme leader's role is that of expert explainer or modeller. Their role is to convey clearly the new learning and its relevance. This might include the process learners need to follow, what the beautiful outcome should look like, the principles learners need to apply, and the difference it will make to their lives and the success of the organisation.

In the *we* stage, the programme leader's role morphs into one of detective and evaluator. They seek direct feedback that the teaching that was delivered in the *me* stage has been received and interpreted in the way it was intended. The *we* stage is a little like the amber traffic light – it is the get-ready-to-go stage. If learners lack clarity or retain misconceptions, then the programme leader may need to move back to the *me* stage to remodel and re-explain in a different way. If, on the other hand, feedback from learners shows that shared clarity exists, then the course leader can move them on to the *you* stage, where they can begin to practise. This is why we refer to the *we* stage as the 'hinge point' in the model.

In the *you* stage, the learners practise or apply the newly acquired KASH, with opportunities for structured feedback from the programme leader and their peers. The programme leader acts as coach at this stage in the model. It is crucially important that the leader only moves those learners who are ready on to the *you* stage. If they move prematurely, without full clarity, learners may well start practising skills incorrectly and embedding bad habits. In addition, the amount of corrective feedback required may well overwhelm some learners. For this reason, we always advise programme leaders to aim for an 80%+ success rate with learners before moving them on to the *you* stage.

In some learning programmes, the *you* stage isn't built into the programme design. However, where knowledge, attitude, skill and habit development are being sought, this is likely to significantly limit the successful embedding of sustainable learning.

In this chapter we will focus on the first two stages of the model. In Chapter 8, we will examine the *you* stage in much more detail.

The *me* stage

In this phase, the programme leader's role is to ensure that the why, the what and the how are explained clearly to learners. The most effective programme leaders make the skill of explaining look effortless. It is not just that they convey complex concepts and ideas coherently, but their carefully sequenced modelling also helps learners to see the bigger picture and how all the separate parts fit together. Instead of feeling cognitively overloaded, learners become clear and confident about their learning. The best programme leaders put a great deal of thought and care into their analysis and planning to ensure learners gain clarity and avoid confusion.

To ensure that the *me* stage does not overwhelm learners' working memory, it is important to carefully plan both the 'big picture' and 'small picture' elements of the programme. The big picture focuses on the overview of the learning: the sequence and structure. The small picture focuses on how the individual elements of new learning are modelled and explained, simply and succinctly.

The 'big picture': designing using the room layout

Whenever we are working to support the development of in-house programme designers or planning our own training, be it keynote speeches or longer-term programmes, we always start with the big picture.[1] The big picture represents the key aspects of KASH that we are seeking to build into the programme.

The aim is to find the most logical sequence in which to deliver the new information. Where is the best place to start? A really useful way to think about the big picture is to think of the learning programme as the room layout of a house. Each room represents a key aspect of the new learning that needs to be explained or modelled. The programme leader takes the learners on a tour through the house. By organising new learning as a progression through a series of rooms, learners are introduced to the new content in a clear and step-by-step way.

Think of the way estate agents take potential clients through a house or apartment. Ask yourself, which is the best room to start in? What sequence of rooms will grab the learners' attention and motivate them? What sequence will provide the most coherent understanding of the new learning?

---

1   It was a key tool in organising the sequencing and writing of this book too.

Below is an example of a room layout for a single session within a longer leadership development programme:

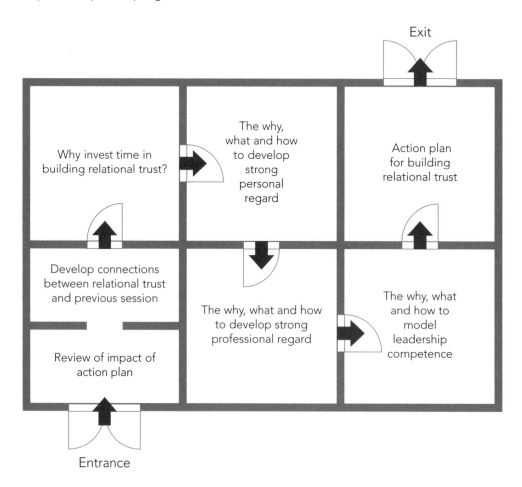

The focus of the session is relational trust. Within each room, the programme leader concentrates on one specific principle. To begin the session, the group review the progress they have made against their individual action plans and the work they have done so far. The review room provides connections back to previous sessions and helps the learners to prepare for moving into the next room, where they make connections with the focus of this session: why invest time in doing this?

If this question can be satisfactorily answered, the chances are that the learners will be motivated to take the rest of the tour. They tackle the why, what and how, followed by a deconstruction of the ingredients for relational trust and the tools and strategies to develop it. The final room is the action planning room where learners have time to reflect and construct an action plan for change.

It is easy to see that the programme designer has used the analogy of room layout to think logically and emotionally about the best way to sequence the learning for the session. When designing your own room layout, remember to make the size of the rooms proportionate to the time you plan to spend there. The process of analysing and then creating the layout can often take several iterations to get right. However, the time spent planning will really help learners to avoid cognitive overload. Room layouts can also be used when planning multi-session learning programmes. In this case, each room would represent an individual session within the whole programme.

It is a really useful reviewing technique to share the room layout with the learners at the start and end of each session so they can understand the big picture for themselves.

Designer action points

Design the room layout for one of your current learning programmes:

In which order would it be best to arrange the tour of these rooms? Where should you go first? Where, logically, would it make sense to go after that?

Is there sufficient time to ensure shared clarity is achieved in each room?

The 'small picture': the skill of modelling and explaining new learning

Sometimes the question, 'How are we going to model and explain this clearly?', can be a neglected aspect of learning programmes. Instead, programme designers can be lured into spending all their planning time organising PowerPoint slideshows and preparing the activities they are going to use with learners. Our strong advice is that planning how the new learning is going to be modelled and explained is far more important. Those who do this well make new learning far easier to grasp than their less expert peers, and learners' progress is faster, particularly those at the lower end of the performance continuum.

What follows is a selection of proven tools and strategies to ensure that you will be able to convey the new learning in your programme as convincingly as possible.

Connecting new learning to what is known already

In Chapter 6, we emphasised the value of establishing well-defined starting points for learners. This provides the programme leader with a massive advantage at the *me* stage. By knowing what learners are already familiar with, programme leaders can use pre-existing knowledge as hooks on which to connect new learning. Indeed, if these hooks are neglected, there is a danger that new learning will be quickly lost.

Analogies and metaphors are excellent ways to draw in and build on the existing knowledge of learners. They enable comparisons to be drawn between different and seemingly disconnected things. You might have noticed that we have used them throughout this book to help us do some of the heavy lifting in terms of making ourselves clear. When modelling new learning, using analogies or metaphors can help learners to connect what is new with what they know already.

Analogies compare the features of two different things and identify what they have in common. One leader used a powerful analogy when he described the difficulty he'd had trying to improve the outcomes in his team without investing time in building their KASH. 'It's like I've been trying to drive at 60 mph in a car stuck in first gear. It's possible but it gives me little control and quickly ruins the engine.'

Metaphors convey much more than a simple comparison between two things – for example, 'He's the black sheep of the family.' A metaphor invites us to consider how a comparison of two unlike things or events deepens our understanding of each. They have the magical quality of communicating the essence of an idea by representing it as something else.

At a training session we led some time ago, the delegates were discussing the meaning of Holocaust survivor Viktor Frankl's quote, 'Man does not simply exist but always decides what his existence will be.'[2] One participant used a metaphor which not only supported her own understanding but also gave instant clarity to her colleagues too: 'Imagine being adrift in the middle of a rough ocean on a life raft. This quote says to me: you have a rudder and a sail. You have the power to change your course by making use of them. Or you can do nothing and stay adrift. That's a choice too.' The metaphor's clarity enabled the group to connect with the central idea of the original quotation and think deeply about whether they were 'deciding beings' themselves.

Metaphors also work well visually. At a presentation we attended recently, a speaker held up two glasses of blackcurrant squash. The squash in the first glass was diluted, and in the second glass it was much more concentrated. She used this visual metaphor to highlight the variable quality of customer service in her organisation, and this helped ensure that her message was effective and memorable.

Designer/programme leader action point

How could you use analogies or metaphors to convey new learning clearly?[3]

---

2   Viktor Frankl, *Man's Search for Meaning* (Boston, MA: Beacon Press, 1992 [1959]), p. 133.
3   You can use metaphors and analogies in the *we* stage too. Challenging learners to create metaphors related to their new learning provides feedback about the quality of their understanding.

The power of story

Stories can be another powerful and 'sticky' way to convey new learning. To emphasise the point, we challenge you to answer the two questions below from earlier in the book – and please, no cheating!

1   In Chapter 1, how many cars did Toyota have to recall as a result of the quality issues they encountered?

2   Who was McArthur Wheeler, and why were his actions relevant to this book?

It is likely that the second answer was far easier to recall than the first.[4] This is probably because the case of Wheeler was presented as a story. Research suggests that storytelling and story listening capacities are hard-wired into the human brain.[5] Stories are the basic way we learn about the world and store information. Additionally, stories link up information in ways that are much more memorable than facts.

The best stories on learning programmes powerfully connect learners with the why, what and how questions. They may illuminate the path to change or, alternatively, highlight the pitfalls ahead that need to be avoided. At their best, stories create empathy between the storyteller and the learner.

It is useful to note, however, that while stories about problems and pitfalls can act as a warning, too much negativity can leave the delegates feeling thoroughly depressed! Most people have a preference for a more positive balance of inspiration and optimism rather than unremitting gloom.

When considering the use of story in your learning programmes, it may be helpful to consider the following questions:

■ What are the key messages I want to get across?

■ Which stories will most effectively carry that message and answer the why, what and how questions required for shared clarity?

■ How will my story help me to build relationships and inspire the learners?

---

4   Toyota recalled 1.66 million vehicles. Wheeler was the bank robber who suffered from a huge perception gap.
5   See Harrison Monarth, 'The Irresistible Power of Storytelling as a Strategic Business Tool', *Harvard Business Review* (11 March 2014). Available at: https://hbr.org/2014/03/the-irresistible-power-of-storytelling-as-a-strategic-business-tool.

We have been in a few training rooms where the use of stories has been a little overdone, so try not to overuse them. This links back to the principle of planning backwards: unless the story is obviously relevant it can create cognitive overload. One delegate confided to us, after one story-packed session, that the presenter had more stories than Billy Connolly. That probably was not the learning outcome that the presenter wanted the delegates to go away with.

Designer/programme leader action point

How could you use story to convey new learning?

Demystifying through positive visualisation

Models, videos, photos and images can really help learners to visualise the intended process and outcome of a learning programme. They can also play a key role in helping learners to answer the why question for themselves, because they will clearly see the difference between their current KASH and the desired one. Starting a learning programme with a visual of the desired outcome also gives learners the big picture (the what) right from the outset. And as learners begin to deconstruct the big picture, they automatically begin to address the how as well. For instance, on a programme designed to improve participants' planning skills, the course leader gave them examples of excellent planning at the outset. This really helped the group to decode the skills, making the process much easier to comprehend.

Designer/programme leader action point

What visual examples are available, or could you create, to make new learning clear?

Visual organisers

We love the simplicity of the London Underground map. Travellers, especially those unfamiliar with the city, can refer to it throughout their journey. It helps them to see how they are progressing, how far they have gone, how many stops they have left and where they need to change train. The map shows how the different stations on the Underground are linked. The Tube map is a classic example of the power of visual organisers to create clarity.

Visual organisers come in a variety of forms. The factor they have in common is that they help learners to easily grasp the interrelationships between new pieces of information. Instead of being overloaded, learners are able to see how the information fits together. One colleague summed them up perfectly when she described them as, 'like the picture on the box of a jigsaw puzzle. It's not impossible to complete a 1,000 piece jigsaw puzzle without looking at it, but it's a lot easier when you can!'

The first visual organiser below helped a programme leader to clearly demonstrate the relationship between causes and effects – in this case, a situation in which relational trust had broken down within a team:

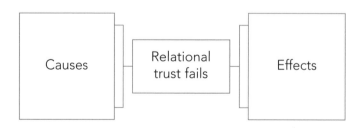

This second visual organiser breaks down a process into a series of manageable steps so that learners are able to see the underlying structure:

A host of different visual organisers can be downloaded free from: www. learningimperative.co.uk/downloads/visual-organisers.

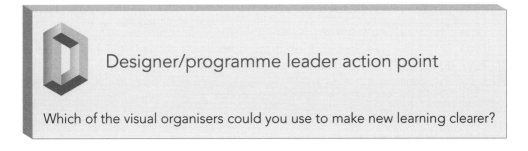

Designer/programme leader action point

Which of the visual organisers could you use to make new learning clearer?

Making time for regular review

Making time and space for learners to review new learning plays a vital role in creating clarity as well as preventing cognitive overload. In multi-session programmes, reviewing is an important strategy to use towards the start of each session. It provides learners with the time to recall and reappraise learning from the previous sessions. This ensures that even the busiest individual has time to stop and consolidate their learning. It also enables learners to be better prepared to hook new learning to what they have covered previously.

Reviewing has huge value within individual sessions too. Reviewing in this context takes the form of opportunities to reflect on key points or new information. The following questions will provide learners with thinking time to make sense of their new learning:

- What are the key learning points from this session?

- What connections do you see between your role and this new learning?

- How are you going to take this new learning forward?

- Which parts of this new learning are you finding most challenging?

- What will you need to start or stop doing in order to improve?

Designer/programme leader action point

Where will you locate the key review points in your room layout? (The regularity of review will depend on how complex and unfamiliar the new learning is.)

The *we* stage

The importance of the *we* stage in achieving shared clarity cannot be overemphasised. There are two main reasons for this. First, the *we* stage enables the programme leader to get feedback about whether delegates have clearly understood the new learning presented during the *me* stage. It is essential that leaders seek the strongest proof possible that shared clarity exists at this point. If it doesn't, now is the time to go back and correct any misconceptions and misunderstandings. Without shared clarity, learners will find it hard to grasp the full implications of the why, what and how, which will negatively affect the impact of the programme.

The second purpose of the *we* stage is to create opportunities for learners to engage in thinking deeply about what they are learning. For learning to be sustainable, the skills and practices need to be transferred to the delegates' long-term memories. Deep thought and reflection are a crucial part of this process, so it is important to consider two fundamental questions:

1   What do I want learners to remember from this programme?

2   How will I make sure there is maximum time to engage in thinking hard about the answer(s) to question 1?

Creating 'prove it' opportunities

A valuable strategy at the *we* stage is to create 'prove it' opportunities through-out the session. Prove it opportunities put backbone into the learning process by challenging learners to demonstrate their understanding of new learning. It is helpful here to refer back to the 'room layout' to consider where these prove it tasks would be best positioned. Typically, we don't want learners moving from one room to another without first proving they have 'got' the learning so far!

Big picture–small picture

Challenge learners to prove it by inviting them to make connections between their new learning (small picture) and the bigger picture of what they know already. One example of this was a session in which learners were challenged to apply their understanding of relational trust to the KASH of an effective coach.

Unpick the problem

Another useful tool is to challenge learners to unpick a problem related to the new learning. There are three ways of using this strategy. The first is to get learn-ers to identify the potential causes of a particular problem. The second is to ask them to pinpoint the likely effects of a problem. The third is to challenge them to identify ways to prevent the problem occurring in the first place. The value of this strategy is that it helps learners to understand potential issues that could arise and how to pre-empt, solve or avoid them. An example of this was a 'train the trainer' programme we participated in some years ago. The presenter posed the following: 'The learners leave the session confused. What might have caused this problem? How can you avoid learners experiencing confusion in your own sessions?'

Apply to a real-life role

This strategy invites learners to identify where and how they could apply their new learning in their role – for example, on a learning designer programme, delegates were asked to apply the room layout tool to a learning programme they were currently designing. This provided opportunities for the delegates to prove their understanding through their use of the tool, and if necessary receive additional support from the course leader.

Using questioning to prompt deeper thinking

Effective questioning is a key ingredient in the *we* stage. Typically, this is questioning that stimulates deep thinking and dialogue, and also exposes potential misunderstandings and areas of confusion. Skilful questioning will also engage learners in developing connections with what they already know.

Use questions such as these to probe for proof of clarity about processes and outcomes:

■ What are the key steps for dealing with this issue?

■ What do we need to consider carefully here?

■ What does … mean?

■ How does this relate to what we have been talking about?

■ What do we already know about this?

■ Can you give me an example of when we could use this?

■ Are you saying … or … ?

■ Could you rephrase that?

Use questions like these to focus thinking on causes and effects:

■ What are the main causes of event X?

■ How can these causes be avoided/mitigated/enhanced?

■ What could be the effects of this?

■ Which of these effects are unique to this situation?

- How might these effects be avoided/enhanced?

- What might be the possible impact of these effects?

- What might happen then?

Use questions like these to seek evidence from learners on their reasoning:

- Tell me more about why are you saying …

- How would we know if this is correct/incorrect?

- What assumptions might have been made here?

- Talk me through your thinking steps …

- Are there any alternative ways of looking at this?

- Why would that happen?

- Are there other ways of looking at this?

- What are the strengths and weaknesses of …?

Use questions like these to prompt for action:

- What are going to be your first steps as a result of today?

- What are the key changes you want to make?

- What options are open to you here?

- Which option are you going to move forward with?

- When will this be completed by?

- What support might you need along the way?

Designer/programme leader action points

Which of the *we* stage tools could be used to elicit deeper thinking as well as proof of understanding?

Which of the questions listed would be useful to obtain proof of learning?

Developing the KASH to be an effective questioner

Where we've worked with programme leaders who have been really effective in leading the *we* stage, they have developed certain key aspects of their own KASH. Indeed, in our experience, the effectiveness or otherwise of the *we* stage is dependent upon on the KASH of the programme leader. Where the individual has these key KASH components, a safe learning environment is created where deep thinking and dialogue is the norm. The most important KASH requirements that programme leaders need are:

- **Knowledge.** They have a clear understanding of the complex aspects of the new learning as well as the potential misconceptions. This helps them to focus conversations on these areas to ensure learners achieve clarity rapidly.

- **Curiosity.** They are innately curious. They ask questions and develop rich dialogue with learners because they are keen to find out who is clear and who isn't. They have a tendency to probe deeply with their questions as they are aware that correct answers don't necessarily signify understanding – for example, the learner might have guessed correctly or got to the right answer using flawed reasoning. Skilful programme leaders ask questions to test for proof of understanding, such as: 'What thinking steps did you use to get that answer?'

- **Interpersonal skills.** They develop a safe environment in which learners can get things wrong or admit they aren't sure. This safe space ensures that questioning is not perceived as threatening. After all, it is hard to get proof if learners are reluctant to answer for fear of making mistakes.

■ **Listening and observing skills.** They have the sensitivity to stop talking and instead really listen to learner feedback, as well as observe the learners applying their understanding. A programme leader who had watched herself facilitate a discussion on video playback was appalled: 'I didn't shut up. I kept interrupting responses from learners and finishing their explanations for them. The only person who had the chance to prove their understanding was me! I've got no proof at all about the group's learning.'

Planning for improvement

The final element of the *we* stage is to find proof that learners are able to apply their new learning. This might be done by observing them in their day-to-day role or, alternatively, it can be achieved during the *you* stage – where 'plus one' challenge and feedback come into play to support development of the desired KASH. We will explore the *you* stage in Chapter 8.

We are big fans of ensuring that sufficient time is available at the end of the programme for learners to plan how they will apply their new learning at work. Don't just assume that new learning will be applied automatically. Not only does learning need time to become embedded, but others in the workplace may feel threatened by change and resist attempts to introduce more effective working practices.

It is essential to blend the clarity provided by the why, what and how with a workable action plan. This plan should provide learners with the step change actions needed to improve their own performance. One way to do this is to use the table on page 196. It challenges learners to identify actions to start and stop, thus helping to avoid cognitive overload. It also links actions with what learners are seeking to achieve. This helps them to see the bigger picture and satisfactorily answer the why question.

As a result of the programme	In order to achieve	Deadline date
I will start …		
I will stop …		
I will do more of …		
I will do less of …		

Where the size of the group allows, creating time for learners to share their individual action plans with each other can help to cultivate peer accountability. Large groups can be split into smaller groups for this purpose. Sharing can also enable learners to identify peers who have similar action plans, which can lead to fruitful opportunities for collaboration and peer support.

REFRESH reading list

Some suggested reading if you want to delve deeper:

Duarte, Nancy (2008). *Slide:ology: The Art and Science of Creating Great Presentations* (Sebastopol, CA: O'Reilly Media).

Owen, Nick (2001). *The Magic of Metaphor: 77 Stories for Teachers, Trainers and Thinkers* (Carmarthen: Crown House Publishing).

Owen, Nick (2004). *More Magic of Metaphor: Stories for Leaders, Influencers, Motivators and Spiral Dynamics Wizards* (Carmarthen: Crown House Publishing).

Reynolds, Garr (2012). *Presentation Zen: Simple Ideas on Presentation Design and Delivery* (Berkeley, CA: New Riders).

Chapter 8

The *you* stage

Practising to go 'plus one'

About twenty years ago, I (Mark) was a keen road runner, competing regularly in half marathons. Running faster and achieving ever better personal best times became an all-consuming passion. Yet, despite training ever harder, sometimes running twice a day, up to fifty miles a week, my performance plateaued. It became dispiriting. And then a chance conversation with a fellow runner provided a 'eureka' moment, a launch pad for improvement. 'I've noticed your times have stagnated recently,' he said. 'Why not come along to our club? I reckon we can help.'

He wasn't wrong. Training at the club was a revelation – it was a radically different and more methodical approach compared to what I had been doing. Previously, training had consisted of going out alone, pounding the pavements at a steady pace for an hour at a time. Yet at the club, it took place on a running track and typically involved a long series of lung-bursting runs, at top speed, for two to three minutes, followed by a short recovery jog. It wasn't a solitary process either. Training was alongside other runners, most of whom were faster than me. This provided the additional challenge of having to keep up. The final ingredient was feedback. This came from the group's excellent coach. He gave pinpoint guidance to each runner on a wide range of areas – from nutrition to recovery, as well as important but less obvious areas such as stride length and breathing patterns. Fast forward twelve months and the new training regime paid off handsomely. More than six minutes had been taken off my personal best time over the half marathon distance!

This is a perfect representation of the *you* stage at its highly effective best: runners taking part in focused and challenging practice sessions supported by targeted feedback on improvement. This learning journey amply demonstrated that the old adage 'practice makes perfect' is only partially true. Practice needs to be the *right* practice. With careful planning and execution, the *you* stage can lead to much more effective results and enhanced performance, while keeping learners more motivated too.

■ Have you ever tried to build the KASH of your team but struggled to achieve real improvement?

■ Are you keen to understand the most effective ways to structure high impact practice for learners?

■ Are you looking for practical ways to ensure that the *you* stage of your learning programme really delivers improved and sustainable performance?

What's in this chapter for me?

This chapter reveals the five key ingredients required when designing or leading the *you* stage of a learning programme. We will explain each ingredient and its importance in turn, and we will outline practical strategies to ensure the ingredients are integrated into your programme. Finally, we will examine the KASH required to lead this stage effectively. By the end of the chapter, you will be equipped to plan and lead effective practice opportunities to develop learners' KASH, as well as ensuring that they want to come back for more.

Why is the *you* stage so important?

For programmes seeking to develop more than just knowledge, the *you* stage is crucial. It is the stage that provides learners with the opportunity to practise and embed new attitudes, skills and habits which the *me* and *we* stages have introduced. Indeed, unless there is a *you* stage in the programme, learners will lack the structured opportunities that directly lead to improvement in their day-to-day performance.

Without the opportunity to practise, they will also lack the valuable chance to get targeted feedback on their efforts. Without a *you* stage, it is a little like trying to become proficient at driving a car simply by watching your instructor drive and reading the Highway Code from cover to cover. The *you* stage puts the learners behind the wheel so they can practise with in-the-moment feedback from their coach. We have seen so many otherwise excellent and engaging learning programmes fail because their designer has overlooked the importance of building in the *you* stage to enable learners to practise.

There are five ingredients which maximise the chances that learners' practice will lead to improved performance. They also inhibit processing overload, low relational trust and perception gaps – the barriers to learning that we described in Part II – thus increasing the chances that learners will practise and succeed. As with baking, all the ingredients, blended together, have a significant impact on the outcome. Consequently, we highly recommend using the self-reflection questions at the end of each section to ensure that each element is present in the *you* stage of your own learning programme.

1. Micro focus

The principles of planning backwards that we detailed in Chapter 6 apply perfectly in micro focus to the *you* stage too – in particular, the importance of creating shared clarity about desired learning outcomes. Learning designers need to be clear on the following two questions: what exactly are we trying to achieve in each practice session, and what will success look like in each session? If the answers to these questions are vague or overly lengthy, the chances are that the *you* stage won't be effective. A sharp and shared micro focus for both coach and learner brings several key benefits, as seen in the following case study.

Case study: focus on deepening dialogue

Michael was keen to improve the way he led his team meetings. He felt his performance often came up short. However, when he sat down with his coach and considered the KASH required to lead meetings more effectively, he was overwhelmed by how many different aspects there were. His coach, in the capacity of programme designer, suggested that he practise improving just one element – the quality of his own questioning of others. With this single focus, Michael was able to concentrate on improving two key factors: first, to be more inclusive in order to draw out contributions from his more introverted team members, and, second, to nurture deeper thinking by asking more open questions.

This micro focus was crucial in helping Michael to improve for the following reasons:

■ Michael avoided processing overload by holding just two questions in the forefront of his mind: how can my questions push deeper thinking (such as those on pages 192–193), and who haven't I heard from?

■ Michael and his coach concentrated only on feedback about what was working and what needed further practice.

■ Michael was able to clearly see how each stage of learning fitted into the overall journey. He and his coach focused their shared thinking on achieving the first target before moving on to the second.

All of which meant that Michael was able to incorporate effective practice into his busy day-to-day routines.

Designer/programme leader action point

What KASH micro focus for practice could you develop for a learning programme that you are currently working on?

2. 'Plus one' challenges

One of the lessons from the story at the beginning of this chapter is the importance of pitching the level of challenge appropriately. Using the runners' race times, the coach was able to place a new arrival into a group of athletes who performed at a similar standard. Had the training group contained international athletes, the chances are that Mark would have quickly lost motivation, seeing his fellow runners disappearing off into the distance. On the other hand, had he been put in a group with much slower athletes, there would have been no challenge to stretch himself. Lack of challenge can also lead to loss of motivation.

Of course, it is unlikely that your programme will take place on a running track, but the importance of challenge in practice at the *you* stage remains. Thus, we advocate what we call 'plus one' challenges. These ensure that every practice session provides the opportunity for the learner to go plus one on their existing level of performance. This ensures that their practice is not too easy, not too hard, but challenging enough for them to have to think deeply about what they are doing as they are doing it. Getting the level of challenge right is crucial because learning takes place when learners are thinking hard. Plus one challenges ensure that learners have to fully concentrate to achieve the micro focus target.

The other significant benefit of plus one challenges is that they create a rich environment for feedback to support learner development. After all, when learners are not struggling to master something new there is little need for feedback and reflection. Johnny, a colleague we worked with a couple of years ago, typified the importance of challenge in his post-programme reflections when he commented: 'The key aspect of the programme was the constant challenge to go plus one and know that a rich learning dialogue would come from it, whether what I did was brilliant or a flop.' Johnny's realisation was that learning is enriched greatly by challenge. He relished the reflection and dialogue which took place afterwards with his coach, especially when practice sessions didn't work out as planned. He found that the discussions, which focused on what to do differently next time, were really powerful. This process fast-tracked his learning and improvement.

In order to manage the level of plus one practice for learners, the coach needs to be clear on three points:

1   The KASH starting point of each learner.

2   The plus one on this level of performance.

3   The improvement advice needed to close the gap between (1) and (2)

Just as we described in Chapter 6, where the learning programme as a whole is focused on closing gaps between the starting point and the desired outcome, so the same process takes place on a micro level at the *you* stage for each learner's individual practice.

Reflection question

Consider a learning programme you have been part of. How clearly defined were the plus one challenges for learners?

Just as individuals at the gym adjust the heaviness of the weights they lift or the speed of the treadmill, according to their own individual fitness level, so programme designers need to adapt the *you* stage for learners at different levels of competence and development.

Designer/programme leader action points

Have you ensured that learners have plus one challenges during the *you* stage on your learning programme?

Have the plus one challenges been pitched appropriately based on the starting points of learners?

3. Iteration

Regular iteration trumps one-off practice, so the third key ingredient is that the learner gets multiple opportunities to encounter plus one challenges and then receives feedback.

When learning programmes only provide one-off opportunities to practise new skills, learners lack sufficient rehearsal time to embed and consolidate their learning. This has several unwanted effects. First, the learner may be left with the residual experience of failure at the end of the programme. If they encountered setbacks during their only opportunity to practise, they may lack confidence when applying their new learning back in their job role.

Second, those who were able to practise effectively during their single opportunity may have a false sense of security. It could well be that their understanding of how and why they were successful is lacking, or it could be that they are unable to translate their learning across different contexts. Either way, it turns out that their effective performance may have been a fluke.

Providing multiple opportunities to practise and refine performance enables valuable ongoing thinking and discussion about the patterns or sequences required to achieve success. As we explained in Chapter 3, this shared clarity is best achieved through dialogue.

Take the experience of learning to drive. Most learner drivers start at the unconsciously incompetent end of the continuum below. In other words, they don't know that they don't know how to drive. After all, for a new driver, driving can look like an effortless task in the hands of an expert – until, of course, they are asked to sit in the driver's seat and are handed the keys. The purpose of iterative practice is that it provides repeated opportunities for learners to practise, get immediate feedback and move along the continuum towards unconscious competence. When learners reach unconscious competence, their coach has effectively made themselves redundant; the learner has developed the required KASH, which means they have reached the high performer level.

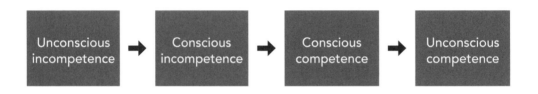

Designer/programme leader action point

Have you designed the *you* stage to provide multiple opportunities for practice and feedback?

4. Plus one feedback

As learners practise, they need regular access to plus one feedback – that is, feedback which helps them to move from one level of performance to the next. This feedback needs to be both accurate and timely.

Accuracy

Many years ago, Andy was given a great piece of advice by a teacher: 'If you want to learn how to do something better, ask someone who has already achieved it.' This was the problem Mark faced as he tried to improve his half marathon performance. Training alone, the only feedback he was getting was from himself. Mark was chasing his own tail. The role of an excellent coach is to offer accurate feedback derived from a wider perspective of theory and experience.

Plus one challenges are usually not enough by themselves. Learners also need access to plus one feedback to support their KASH development. Over time, they will progressively become able to provide this feedback for themselves. However, in the meantime, they can benefit by having a coach to fast-track their improvement, especially by developing their capacity for accurate self-feedback. Again, learning to drive provides the perfect analogy: while it may be possible for someone to discover how to drive through trial and error, it will be much quicker and safer to have an instructor alongside them to provide immediate and expert feedback. This feedback needs to pinpoint exactly what changes the learner needs to apply – step by step – to move to the next level of performance.

A key element of plus one feedback is that it focuses on planning backwards – from the ability of learners to give themselves accurate self-feedback. When coaches do this well they make themselves redundant. If they don't, learners will remain dependent on others for their performance. The central role of the coach is to build the capacity of learners to solve problems for themselves.

Timeliness

One of our clients exhibited a major flaw in the way their plus one feedback was provided. Learners had many opportunities to practise, but they often had to wait for more than a week for feedback on their performance. This time lag meant that the value of the feedback dropped sharply. When they finally sat down with their coach to discuss the session, many couldn't remember the details as so much else had happened in the meantime. It was particularly tough for those learners whose practice sessions had not gone well. They had to stew on the issues for several days until they were able to unpick them with their coach.

Therefore, we strongly advise that feedback is given as close to the practice session as possible for two important reasons. First, when feedback is given in a timely way, learners can use it immediately to improve their performance. In some cases, training sessions can be interrupted for in-the-moment feedback using techniques such as 'time outs' or 'pause buttons'. For example, in one training session, the coach asked the learner to pause, look around her and notice if anything was missing. The learner immediately realised that she had overlooked a crucial stage in the process and was able to correct it there and then. This enabled the practice to continue successfully. Afterwards, the dialogue focused on how the learner could access a visual cue to remember this stage of the process in the future.

The second point is that when feedback is immediate, or at least follows straight after the training session, the coach can utilise the feedback to further refine the learner's plus one challenge for the next session. After all, feedback is a two-way street. At its best, it provides information for learners about ways to improve, as well as information for the coach about how the learner is progressing and what is the next useful logical step.

Designer/programme leader action points

Does the feedback learners receive consistently provide them with the guidance to move their existing performance on plus one?

Have you ensured that immediate feedback is available to guide improvement?

5. REFRESH

The impact of practice is hugely enhanced when both learner and coach commit to the REFRESH characteristics wholeheartedly. It is therefore necessary to create a shared understanding of this from the outset.

The coach and the learner need to work together to discover the processes and practices that have made the *you* stage effective. With each of the REFRESH characteristics below, we offer questions for the coach and the learner to reflect on, both generally and specifically in terms of how and why the *you* stage has been successful in improving their performance. The aim is to ensure that both coach and learner evaluate how the process they have been through has ensured progress, rather than just focusing on the outcome.

REFRESH characteristic	Coach reflection questions	Learner reflection questions
Resilience	■ Where do opportunities exist for learners to reflect on the relationship between learning from setbacks and later success? ■ How am I helping learners to recognise the role that resilience plays in their ability to overcome obstacles?	■ What have I learned about my own resilience through the course of the programme?
Enquiring	■ How am I using open questions to stimulate deeper reflection and analysis of learner performance? ■ In what ways can I nurture the curiosity of learners through the practice stage?	■ What could be my next learning steps? ■ Where, in the future, might I utilise this spirit of enquiry?

REFRESH characteristic	Coach reflection questions	Learner reflection questions
Feedback	■ How am I modelling the characteristics of effective feedback that is kind, specific and helpful (see Chapter 5)? ■ How am I helping learners to reflect on the connection between acting on feedback and their subsequent improvement? ■ How am I seeking feedback from learners about the quality of the feedback they are receiving from me?	■ What was it about the feedback I received that helped me? ■ Were there any points at which the feedback I received failed to help? ■ Where might I find sources of quality feedback that I can draw on in the future?
Revising	■ Where do opportunities exist to reflect on ways that revision has led to improved performance? ■ How am I encouraging greater openness to change? ■ How can I encourage greater risk taking in order to grow positive mindsets?	■ What were the key changes I made that helped my performance to improve? ■ How has my thinking changed over the course of the programme?

REFRESH characteristic	Coach reflection questions	Learner reflection questions
Effortful	■ How am I signposting the value of the effort required to practise effectively? ■ How am I recognising the effort that each learner is making to improve through practice?	■ Where have I had to focus most effort in order to improve?
Sharing	■ How does the practice ensure a two-way sharing of ideas and an understanding of ways to improve? ■ How can I engineer effective collaboration between learners on the programme?	■ What have I learned most from others taking part in the programme? ■ Where could there be other opportunities for collaboration in the future?
Habitual	■ How am I nurturing an appreciation of the need for practice to become a habitual performance boosting activity?	■ How can I maintain the improvements I have made so they become ingrained habits? ■ Which habits have been the hardest to change? Why?

REFRESH characteristic	Coach reflection questions	Learner reflection questions
Habitual *cont*	■ How am I ensuring that the *you* stage exemplifies the importance of creating sustained improvement through changes in habits?	

Not only does REFRESH underpin the *you* stage, but it should – as we plan backwards from a beautiful outcome – give the learner a desire for more of the same. Ideally, we want the programme to enthuse even the most closed-to-learning colleagues because they have experienced for themselves the impact of a well-designed learning programme on their competence and confidence.

The KASH to lead the *you* stage effectively

The final essential ingredient in a successful *you* stage is the coach, who holds together each of the previous ingredients.

We have had the privilege of working alongside a great group of coaches over the past eight years. The way they have consistently supported performance improvement in others through the *you* stage has helped us to pinpoint the most important aspects of the KASH required. The coach's KASH will hugely influence the pace of learners' improvement and, as a consequence, their motivation to persist with their practice. In this section we will outline the key KASH aspects.

Knowledge

A false paradigm exists in some organisations whereby individuals have been selected to coach others solely on the basis of high performance in their day-to-day job. The KASH of a high performing coach can be very different from that required for other roles.

An expert coach must have the ability to deconstruct the KASH of a high performer in a particular discipline and break it down into a series of manageable steps for the learner. This analysis can be difficult for those selected to become a coach based solely on high performance in their field, because they can be too close to their role to be able to see objectively what they do. They aren't clear on why they perform so well because much of it has become an unconscious habit over time. As we described back in Chapter 2, much of what represents high performance is often invisible; therefore, the skill of the effective coach is to analyse and unpick the invisible and make it visible.

An effective coach will also need a good understanding of the learning process in order to develop strong relational trust with the learners. They will also need to understand the best ways to work with learners to support their development throughout the process.

Attitudes

The most effective coaches retain an unswerving belief that anyone, with effective practice, can become a better performer, regardless of their starting point. This is different to the delusional belief that everyone can be world class at everything. Instead, these coaches nurture the attitude in their learners that the focus is on beating their existing personal best – in other words, becoming a better version of themselves. Competing with yourself is a much more psychologically effective process than comparing yourself with others.

Coupled with the belief that improvement can be achieved by all, these coaches habitually question themselves when ongoing practice does not yield improvement. They reflect on their own contribution to the lack of progress and how they can modify their approach in order to kick-start change. It would be far easier to blame the learner and wash their hands of responsibility, but the qualities of resilience and enquiry are also required by the coach.

An example of this enquiring approach is well demonstrated by a coach we know. She has three questions which she asks herself at the end of every programme: what have I learned about building the KASH of a high performer through this programme? What have I learned about the learners during the course of this programme? What have the learners learned as a result of this programme? She is keen to ensure that she has answers, not just to the last question, but to all of them. After all, she is modelling the REFRESH characteristics because she is a learner in the process too.

The final desirable attitudinal trait is the drive of coaches to make themselves redundant by the end of the programme. This is because, by equipping the learners with the KASH they need to sustainably maintain their higher level of performance, they are no longer needed themselves.

Skills

The two skills which are key to supporting the development of learners in the *you* stage are asking specific questions and listening carefully.

Excellent questions are crucial to developing and deepening learners' thinking before and after their practice.

Planning questions to ask before practising include:

- Right now, what choices do you have?
- What are the pros and cons of each option?
- Which option do you prefer?
- In what ways is this option the best choice?
- Are there any other ways of looking at this?
- What key changes will you be making in order to improve?

Reflection questions to ask after practising include:

■ What did/didn't work?

■ What were the reasons for the outcome?

■ What have you learned from practising?

■ What would have been the ideal outcome?

■ What do you need to do next?

■ When are you going to do it?

These questions challenge learners to analyse more deeply the thinking pro-cesses they have used, as well as inviting them to consider other ways to improve.

Effective questions coupled with careful listening provide the coach with valuable feedback in terms of what has been understood and where the learner may need further modelling or feedback. As we mentioned earlier, the aim is to create learner autonomy. The skills of asking good questions and carefully listening to the answers provide coaches with important information about how close or how far the learners are from achieving self-sufficiency.

Habits

The habit that we have noticed most clearly in the coaches we have worked with is their ongoing commitment to the possibility and potential that learning brings. This shines through in their day-to-day application of the knowledge, attitudes and skills outlined above, and not just with others, but also in their dedication to deepening their own learning. As a consequence, there is a humility and energy to their work that fully engages others.

It's never too late for learning

Of all the challenges that accompany the leading of learning programmes, the *you* stage can be the most cognitively demanding, but also by far the most rewarding. It is always a privilege to support the learning and development of others. Building trust, helping them to improve their skills and sometimes even supporting them to overcome psychological barriers, make this a thoroughly worthwhile journey. There is nothing like seeing the look of developing confidence appearing in a learner's eyes and demeanour as they enter the next stage of their professional life with a renewed sense of self-worth and fulfilment.

This transformation was typified by a colleague we worked with nearly ten years ago. We asked her to reflect on the impact of our programme on her performance. She said there had been massive gains, even though the programme had caused her huge personal angst. We were surprised about the angst as she had seemed so engaged all the way through. But then she went on to explain the reason. Just before the programme started, she had felt totally disaffected and had applied for an early retirement scheme. However, over the course of the programme, she had rediscovered her love for the job and all the things that made it worthwhile for her. She realised that she still had much more to offer. The very next day she began her search for a vacancy in a similar role elsewhere! She had experienced the value and imperative of learning on a very personal level.

REFRESH reading list

Some suggested reading if you want to delve deeper:

Ericsson, Anders and Pool, Robert (2017). *Peak: How All of Us Can Achieve Extraordinary Things* (New York: Vintage Books).

Landsberg, Max (2015). *The Tao of Coaching: Boost Your Effectiveness at Work by Inspiring and Developing Those Around You* (London: Profile Books).

Syed, Matthew (2010). *Bounce: The Myth of Talent and the Power of Practice* (London: Fourth Estate).

Whitmore, John (2017). *Coaching for Performance: The Principles and Practice of Coaching and Leadership*, 5th edn (London and Boston, MA: Nicholas Brealey).

Conclusion

Our aim in writing this book has been to provide leaders with a highly practical guide to developing performance through effective learning. Perhaps the question that arises for you now is, what next?

It is clear to see how much many of the leaders we have worked with or interviewed have gained. They recounted stories of jaded colleagues and team members who rediscovered their love of learning and personal development. Individuals who had been apprehensive about trying new ideas because of fear of failure were now embracing a more enquiring and dynamic approach. Team members who never thought they could become high performers surprised themselves with their latent capacities to acquire new skills and confidence. Leaders who themselves had made great breakthroughs in their own learning and self-awareness.

While every leader's story was different, a common thread runs through their narratives: the potential of what is possible for self and others. Learning has provided each one of them with the possibility of a better tomorrow for them and their teams: the possibility of personal and professional growth, the possibility of greater enjoyment and motivation, the possibility of increased competence. What possibilities could high impact learning bring you?

Of course, this isn't to suggest that developing a high performing learning team is easy or without some risks. Some of the following questions may have arisen in your own mind during the course of the book:

- What if building relational trust within my team proves challenging?

- What are the potential risks in holding difficult and courageous conversations?

- What if feedback from the surveys is overwhelmingly negative?

- How do I handle negative voices when I create opportunities for open dialogue in meetings?

These questions demonstrate that this book's key messages about learning are not just limited to the teams we lead. If we are totally committed to the potential and possibilities that high impact learning can bring, then we will do well to address and overcome the doubts or fears that will inevitably arise in our own professional lives.

If we wish our teams to be open to learning, we must model being open to learning ourselves. The REFRESH characteristics apply just as much to leaders as to our teams. In the challenges ahead, we will inevitably need resilience, effortfulness, feedback, opportunities to revise and enquire, and habitual sharing on a day-to-day basis to create the impactful learning culture this book has sought to explore. The lessons from *The Learning Imperative* about designing effective learning for our teams therefore apply equally to ourselves.

Appendix 1: Feedback survey

Questions 1–22 work on a sliding scale of: strongly agree, agree, disagree and strongly disagree. We include a 'Don't know' in case there is a new team member.

Please indicate the extent to which you agree or disagree with the following statements:

1   There is shared clarity about the processes to be followed and what 'excellent' performance looks like in our team.

2   Workload is a major barrier to developing shared clarity in our team.

3   There are significant inefficiencies in how our team works which make improving what we do difficult.

4   There are sufficient opportunities to discuss how the team is performing/ identify areas to develop.

5   Expectations of performance are clear in our team.

6   Feedback from colleagues is helpful in closing performance gaps.

7   We are effective in prioritising our time to address all important tasks.

8   High quality dialogue in our team helps to develop a deeper 'shared language' for the things that we do.

Questions 1–8 seek to gain feedback on:

■ The level of processing overload in the team.

■ The extent to which there is shared clarity in the team.

■ Whether inefficiency/lack of time is a barrier to improvement.

■ Whether dialogue in the team feeds shared clarity or not.

■ Whether feedback is helpful/clear in helping others to improve what they do.

9   Colleagues in the team who deliver high performance are recognised.

10   I believe relational trust in our team is strong.

11   I challenge myself based on professional conversations I have with others.

12   Colleagues constructively challenge me during professional conversations.

13   Time is made for listening to others in our team.

14   There is a culture of honesty and truthfulness in our team.

15   Colleagues in the team feel valued and respected.

16   Problems/setbacks are openly shared in our team.

Questions 9–16 seek to gain feedback on:

■ The level of trust in the team.

■ The level of honesty and truthfulness in the team.

■ The extent to which colleagues feel recognised and valued.

17   There is a culture of open accountability in our team.

18   Colleagues are clear on their own performance level compared to the expected level.

19   Our team is consistently 'open to learning' in seeking to improve our performance.

20   There are sufficient opportunities to learn about the impact of colleagues/ other teams to help improve my own performance.

21   Our team doesn't make the mistake of 'over-assuming' when problem solving.

22   In our team there is a tendency to externalise blame when things go wrong.

Questions 17–22 seek to gain feedback on:

■ The level of open dialogue about improvement.

■ How open and honest the team is about mistakes/setbacks.

■ The extent to which open accountability exists.

■ Whether colleagues have opportunities to identify any perception gaps about their own performance.

■ Whether the team is open to learning.

Please complete the following statement:

23   The three most important changes that I believe would help our team to be more 'open to learning' are:

This free and anonymised survey tool is also available online at: http://www.learningimperative.co.uk/learning-survey.

Appendix 2:
Learning programme planner

The gap	The me stage	The we stage
Destination	*How will shared clarity be created with learners?*	*How will learners demonstrate that they are ready to apply the new learning?*
What specific aspects of learners' KASH will the programme develop?	**Why?**	
K:		
A:		
	What?	**The you stage**
S:		*How will learners be supported to effectively embed the new aspects of KASH in their role?*
H:		
Starting points	**How?**	
How will the starting points of learners be established?		

Bibliography

Achor, Shawn (2010). *The Happiness Advantage: How a Positive Brain Fuels Success in Work and Life* (New York: Crown Business).

Adams, Linda (n.d.). 'Learning a New Skill is Easier Said Than Done', *Gordon Training International*. Available at: http://www.gordontraining.com/free-workplace-articles/learning-a-new-skill-is-easier-said-than-done/.

Beilock, Sian (2011). 'The Curse of Expertise', *Psychology Today* (23 March). Available at: https://www.psychologytoday.com/gb/blog/choke/201103/the-curse-expertise.

Belludi, Nagesh (2010). 'The Halo and Horns Effects (Rating Errors)', *RightAttitudes.com* (30 April). Available at: http://www.rightattitudes.com/2010/04/30/rating-errors-halo-effect-horns-effect.

Berger, Ron (2003). *An Ethic of Excellence: Building a Culture of Craftsmanship with Students* (Portsmouth, NH: Heinemann).

Berney, Catherine (2014). *The Enlightened Organization: Executive Tools and Techniques from the World of Organizational Psychology* (London: Kogan Page).

Block, Peter (2009). *Community: The Structure of Belonging* (San Francisco, CA: Berrett-Koehler).

Brown, Peter C., Roediger, Henry L. and McDaniel, Mark A. (2014). *Make It Stick: The Science of Successful Learning* (Cambridge, MA: Harvard University Press).

Carroll, Lewis (2015 [1896]). *Alice's Adventures in Wonderland* (London: Penguin Random House).

Covey, Stephen M. R. and Merrill, Rebecca (2006). *The Speed of Trust: The One Thing That Changes Everything* (New York: Simon & Schuster).

Covey, Stephen R. (1989). *The 7 Habits of Highly Effective People* (London: Simon & Schuster).

Csikszentmihalyi, Mihaly and Csikszentmihalyi, Isabella Selega (1992). *Optimal Experience: Psychological Studies of Flow in Consciousness* (New York: Cambridge University Press).

de Bono, Edward (2006 [1982]). *De Bono's Thinking Course: Powerful Tools to Transform Your Thinking* (London: BBC Active).

Digman, John M. (1990). 'Personality Structure: Emergence of the Five-Factor Model', *Annual Review of Psychology*, 41(1), 417–440.

Duarte, Nancy (2008). *Slide:ology: The Art and Science of Creating Great Presentations* (Sebastopol, CA: O'Reilly Media).

Duhigg, Charles (2012). *The Power of Habit: Why We Do What We Do, and How to Change* (London: Random House).

Dunning, David, Johnson, Kerri, Ehrlinger, Joyce and Kruger, Justin (2003). 'Why People Fail to Recognize Their Own Incompetence', *Current Directions in Psychological Science*, 12(3), 83–87.

Ericsson, Anders and Pool, Robert (2017). *Peak: How All of Us Can Achieve Extraordinary Things* (New York: Vintage Books).

Exman, Eugene (1952). 'God's Own Man' [interview with Albert Schweitzer], *United Nations World Magazine*, 6(1).

Fisher, Roger and Ury, William (2012). *Getting to Yes: Negotiating an Agreement Without Giving in* (New York: Random House Business).

Frankl, Viktor (1992 [1959]). *Man's Search for Meaning* (Boston, MA: Beacon Press).

Fullan, Michael (2014). *The Principal: Three Keys to Maximizing Impact* (San Francisco, CA: Jossey-Bass).

Goleman, Daniel (2004). *Emotional Intelligence and Working with Emotional Intelligence* (London: Bloomsbury).

Greiling Keane, Angela and Kitamura, Makiko (2010). 'Toyota Credibility Gap on Recalls Sunk in After President's Visit to US', *Bloomberg News* (10 May).

Grote, Dick (2011). 'Let's Abolish Self-Appraisal', *Harvard Business Review* (11 July). Available at: https://hbr.org/2011/07/lets-abolish-self-appraisal.

Hattie, John and Yates, Gregory C. R. (2014). *Visible Learning and the Science of How We Learn* (Abingdon: Routledge).

Herzberg, Frederick, Mausner, Bernard and Snyderman, Barbara Bloch (2011). *Motivation to Work* (London and New Brunswick, NJ: Transaction Publishers).

Hoffer, Eric (1972). *Reflections on the Human Condition* (New York: Harper & Row).

Johnson, Whitney (2018). *Build an A-Team: Play to Their Strengths and Lead Them Up the Learning Curve* (Boston, MA: Harvard Business Review Press).

Kahneman, Daniel (2011). *Thinking, Fast and Slow* (London: Penguin).

Kegan, Robert and Lahey, Lisa Laskow (2009). *Immunity to Change: How to Overcome It and Unlock the Potential in Yourself and Your Organization* (Boston, MA: Harvard Business Review Press).

Kirschner, Paul A., Sweller, John and Clark, Richard E. (2006). 'Why Minimal Guidance During Instruction Does Not Work: An Analysis of the Failure of Constructivist, Discovery, Problem-Based, Experiential, and Inquiry-Based Teaching', *Educational Psychologist*, 41(2), 75–86.

Kline, Nancy (1999). *Time to Think: Listening to Ignite the Human Mind* (London: Cassell Illustrated).

Klingberg, Torkel (2009). *The Overflowing Brain: Information Overload and the Limits of Working Memory*, tr. Neil Betteridge (New York: Oxford University Press).

Kruger, Justin and Dunning, David (1999). 'Unskilled and Unaware of It: How Difficulties in Recognizing One's Own Incompetence Lead to Inflated Self-Assessments', *Journal of Personality and Social Psychology*, 77(6), 1121–1134.

Landsberg, Max (2015). *The Tao of Coaching: Boost Your Effectiveness at Work by Inspiring and Developing Those Around You* (London: Profile Books).

Lash, Joseph P. (1980). *Helen and Teacher: The Story of Helen Keller and Anne Sullivan Macy* (New York: Delacorte Press/Seymour Lawrence).

Lencioni, Patrick M. (2002). *The Five Dysfunctions of a Team: A Leadership Fable* (J-B Lencioni Series) (San Francisco, CA: Jossey-Bass).

Levitin, Daniel (2015). *The Organized Mind: Thinking Straight in the Age of Information Overload* (New York: Penguin).

Lewis, Clive Staples (1998 [1995]). *The Magician's Nephew* (London: Harper Collins Publishers).

Liker, Jeffrey K. (2004). *The Toyota Way: 14 Management Principles from the World's Greatest Manufacturer* (Columbus, OH: McGraw-Hill Education).

Mack, Arien and Rock, Irvin (1998). *Inattentional Blindness* (Cambridge, MA: MIT Press).

Maister, David, Galford, Robert and Green, Charles (2002). *The Trusted Advisor* (London: Simon & Schuster).

Malley, Frank (1999). 'Pele, the Perfect Player', *The Independent* (23 December). Available at: https://www.independent.co.uk/sport/football/international/pele-the-perfect-player-743002.html.

Marcum, David and Smith, Steven (2007). *Egonomics: What Makes Ego Our Greatest Asset (Or Most Expensive Liability)* (New York: Simon & Schuster).

Maslow, Abraham H. (1943). 'A Theory of Human Motivation', *Psychological Review*, 50(4), 370–396.

Metcalfe, Janet and Shimamura, Arthur P. (1994). *Metacognition: Knowing About Knowing* (Cambridge, MA: MIT Press).

Monarth, Harrison (2014). 'The Irresistible Power of Storytelling as a Strategic Business Tool', *Harvard Business Review* (11 March). Available at: https://hbr.org/2014/03/the-irresistible-power-of-storytelling-as-a-strategic-business-tool.

Newport, Cal (2016). *Deep Work: Rules for Focused Success in a Distracted World* (London: Piatkus).

Nin, Anaïs (1961). *Seduction of the Minotaur* (Chicago, IL: Swallow Press).

Nisbett, Richard E. and Wilson, Timothy D. (1977). 'The Halo Effect: Evidence for Unconscious Alteration of Judgments', *Journal of Personality and Social Psychology*, 35(4), 250–256.

O'Hara, Carolyn (2014). 'Proven Ways to Earn Your Employees' Trust', *Harvard Business Review* (27 June). Available at: https://hbr.org/2014/06/proven-ways-to-earn-your-employees-trust.

Observer, The (2014). 'Daniel Kahneman Changed the Way We Think About Thinking. But What Do Other Thinkers Think of Him?' (16 February). Available at: https://www.theguardian.com/science/2014/feb/16/daniel-kahneman-thinking-fast-and-slow-tributes.

Owen, Nick (2001). *The Magic of Metaphor: 77 Stories for Teachers, Trainers and Thinkers* (Carmarthen: Crown House Publishing).

Owen, Nick (2004). *More Magic of Metaphor: Stories for Leaders, Influencers, Motivators and Spiral Dynamics Wizards* (Carmarthen: Crown House Publishing).

Palmer, Alan (2014). *Talk Lean: Shorter Meetings. Quicker Results. Better Relations.* (Chichester: John Wiley).

Patterson, Kerry, Grenny, Joseph, Maxfield, David, McMillan, Ron and Switzler, Al (2013). *Crucial Accountability: Tools for Resolving Violated Expectations, Broken Commitments, and Bad Behavior*, 2nd edn (Columbus, OH: McGraw Hill Education).

Pink, Daniel H. (2010). *Drive: The Surprising Truth About What Motivates Us* (Edinburgh: Canongate).

Plous, Scott (1993). *The Psychology of Judgment and Decision Making* (Columbus, OH: McGraw-Hill Education).

Radcliffe, Steve (2012). *Leadership: Plain and Simple*, 2nd edn (Harlow: Pearson Education).

Reynolds, Garr (2012). *Presentation Zen: Simple Ideas on Presentation Design and Delivery* (Berkeley, CA: New Riders).

Rogers, Carl (1956). *Client-Centered Therapy*, 3rd edn (Boston, MA: Houghton Mifflin).

Roper, Jenny (2016). 'Organisations Must Prepare for Rapid Pace of Change', *HR Magazine* (11 March). Available at: http://hrmagazine.co.uk/article-details/organisations-must-prepare-for-rapid-pace-of-change.

Rosenberg, Marshall B. (2015). *Nonviolent Communication: A Language for Life* (Encinitas, CA: Puddle Dancer Press).

Rotter, J. B. (1966). 'Generalized Expectancies for Internal Versus External Control of Reinforcement', *Psychological Monographs: General & Applied*, 80(1), 1–28.

Rubio, Justin (2012). 'Google Ventures' Joe Kraus: "We're Creating a Culture of Distraction" ', *The Verge* (29 May). Available at: https://www.theverge.com/2012/5/29/3050625/google-ventures-joe-kraus-culture-distractions-presentation.

Schein, Edgar H. (2011). *Helping: How to Offer, Give, and Receive Help* (San Francisco, CA: Berrett-Koehler).

Schein, Edgar H. (2013). *Humble Inquiry: The Gentle Art of Asking Instead of Telling* (San Francisco, CA: Berrett-Koehler).

Senge, Peter (1990). *The Fifth Discipline: The Art and Practice of the Learning Organization* (London and Boston, MA: Nicholas Brealey).

Senge, Peter, Kleiner, Art, Roberts, Charlotte, Ross, Richard B. and Smith, Bryan (2010 [1994]). *The Fifth Discipline Fieldbook: Strategies and Tools for Building a Learning Organization* (London: Nicholas Brealey).

Simon, Herbert A. and Gilmartin, Kevin J. (1973). 'A Simulation Memory for Chess Positions', *Cognitive Psychology*, 5(1), 29–46.

Staats, Bradley R. (2018). *Never Stop Learning: Stay Relevant, Reinvent Yourself and Thrive* (Boston, MA: Harvard Business Review Press).

Stone, Douglas and Heen, Sheila (2015). *Thanks for the Feedback: The Science* and Art of Receiving Feedback Well (New York: Portfolio Penguin).

Sweller, John (1994). 'Cognitive Load Theory, Learning Difficulty, and Instructional Design', *Learning and Instruction*, 4(4), 295–312.

Syed, Matthew (2010). *Bounce: The Myth of Talent and the Power of Practice* (London: Fourth Estate).

Syed, Matthew (2015). *Black Box Thinking: The Surprising Truth About Success* (London: John Murray).

Thorndike, Edward Lee (1920). 'A Constant Error in Psychological Ratings', *Journal of Applied Psychology*, 4(1), 25–29.

Whitmore, John (2017). *Coaching for Performance: The Principles and Practice of Coaching and Leadership*, 5th edn (London and Boston, MA: Nicholas Brealey).

Wiggins, Grant and McTighe, Jay (2005). *Understanding by Design* (Alexandria, VA: Association for Supervision and Curriculum Development).

Zenger, Jack and Folkman, Joseph (2017). 'How Managers Drive Results and Employee Engagement at the Same Time', *Harvard Business Review* (19 June). Available at: https://hbr.org/2017/06/how-managers-drive-results-and-employee-engagement-at-the-same-time.

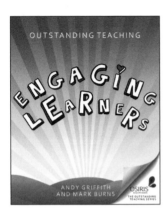

Outstanding Teaching

Engaging Learners

Andy Griffith and Mark Burns

ISBN: 978-184590797-6

Outstanding Teaching: Engaging Learners is based on five years of intensive research through Osiris Educational's award-winning Outstanding Teaching Intervention programme, during which the authors have trained more than 500 teachers to teach over 1,300 lessons in schools nationwide. This book is packed with proven advice and innovative tools developed in these successful outstanding lessons.

Written in the same humorous, thought-provoking style with which they both teach and train, Andy and Mark aim to challenge all who teach, from NQTs to seasoned professionals, to reflect on their day-to-day practice and set an agenda for sustainable teacher and leadership improvement.

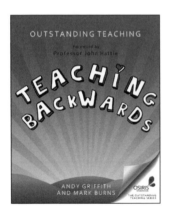

Outstanding Teaching

Teaching Backwards

Andy Griffith and Mark Burns

ISBN: 978-184590929-1

Outstanding Teaching: Teaching Backwards is the follow-up to the bestselling *Outstanding Teaching: Engaging Learners*. It is based on the analysis of thousands of hours of primary and secondary lessons, part of Osiris Educational's Outstanding Teaching Intervention programme over the course of seven years.

Teachers need resources that are clear, concise, and practical. *Teaching Backwards* is just that. It's packed with case studies from primary and secondary teachers, and it's punctuated with reflective questions that invite teachers to slow down and do some thinking about how they currently teach. Well-informed by research and with a clear action plan of what to do, and what not to do, *Teaching Backwards* is a guide to ensuring that learners make outstanding progress, lesson by lesson and year on year.